Coming Together—Coming Apart

JAY KUTEN

Coming Together—Coming Apart

ON ANGER AND SEPARATION IN SEXUAL LOVING

MACMILLAN PUBLISHING CO., INC.

NEW YORK

COLLIER MACMILLAN PUBLISHERS

LONDON

To Susan, with love

*The case histories presented in this book are fiction-
alized composites of cases known to the author. Great
care has been taken to insure that the identity of the
patients remains concealed and therefore all of the
names, occupations, residences, and family relations
have been changed.*

LIBRARY OF CONGRESS CATALOGING IN PUBLICATION DATA

Kuten, Jay.
    Coming together—coming apart; on anger and
separation in sexual loving.

    1. Sex. 2. Marriage. 3. Interpersonal relations.
I. Title.
HQ31.K87   301.41   73–1961
ISBN 0–02–567000–X

Macmillan Publishing Co., Inc.
866 Third Avenue, New York, N.Y. 10022
Collier-Macmillan Canada Ltd.

First Printing 1974

Printed in the United States of America

Contents

That's the Way I've Always Heard It Should Be

My father sits the night with no lights on
His cigarette glows in the dark
The living room is still
I walk by—no remark.

I tiptoe past the master bedroom where
My mother reads her magazines.
I hear her call, "sweet dreams,"
But I forget how to dream.

But you say it's time we moved in together
And raised a family of our own, you and me.
Well, that's the way I've always heard it should be.
You want to marry me ... We'll marry.

My friends from college, they're all married now
They have their houses and their lawns,
They have their silent noons, tearful nights, angry dawns.
Their children hate them for the things they're not.
They hate themselves for what they are ...
And yet, they drink, they laugh,
Close the wound, hide the scar ...

But you say it's time we moved in together
And raised a family of our own, you and me.

Well, that's the way I've always heard it should be.
You want to marry me ... We'll marry.
You say that we can keep our love alive
Babe, all I know is what I see
The couples cling and claw
And drown in love's debris
You say we'll soar like two birds through the clouds,
But soon you'll cage me on your shelf.
I'll never learn to be just me first—by myself ...

Well, Okay, it's time we moved in together
And raised a family of our own, you and me.
Well, that's the way I've always heard it should be ...
You want to marry me ...
                              marry.
                    We'll marry.

Preface

TODAY WE BELIEVE we know a great deal about human sexuality, and yet it remains a mystery. The last decade has brought us dozens of books, hundreds of articles, a veritable snowfall of words—all about sex. Not to mention the plays and the films. There has been so much exposure in the media that it almost seems that the topic must be exhausted. Now that the explicit sex act has become commonplace on the screen, what else is there left to see? Now that the "experts" have told us all we want to know, what else is there left to say?

Supposedly we've undergone a "sexual revolution" in the past ten years. I say "supposedly," for if there's been a revolution, just what are its signs? A lot of grownups look at the apparent casualness with which their kids live *their* sexual lives and feel a sense of envy. They feel a sense of disappointment with their own present lives and a sense of loss of the opportunities in their past. And a lot of kids find that their so-called sexual freedom is a game made up by the media. They may be having sex more often and sooner and more openly. But all it has done is made the problems of sexuality more visible.

The answers change; the questions remain the same.

With all the exposure and factual enlightenment, you might think that a group of mature people could sit down and discuss sexuality in the serious manner they can dispose of any other subject, from conservation to racism. But it is not so easy. Try it, if you care to, with your friends. The conversation quickly breaks down in nervous laughter or gets strangled in distraction and can be maintained at all only with strenuous effort. Unlike sexuality, those other topics can be made abstract, can provide a shield of intellection to hide behind. Sexuality, taken seriously, exposes the bias of personal experience for anyone who tries to deal with it. Beyond the bias, we are mostly unprepared to think seriously about it.

I'm not talking about telling dirty jokes, or smirking over someone's sexual exploits, but about sharing in the problems and pleasures of sexual living, especially the problems.

We're supposed to have pleasure now. It is as though a new commandment has been promulgated in our society: Thou shalt have sexual pleasure. And yet, how come—after all the talk about sexual revolution, after we've stopped asking, "Should we or shouldn't we?"—we frequently end up asking, "Why bother?"

The promise of fulfillment in sexual loving ends too often as a broken dream. And the experts haven't done much more than tell us to dream on. A few have promised us everything—and delivered, in a shroud of flippancy, only confusion and ignorance.

Some have done truly important work. Masters and Johnson have helped to dispel the myths we learned from

our buddies on the street. They and Kinsey before them
have made a serious attempt to elucidate the "facts" of
sexual behavior. And then they couched their knowledge
in such technical language as to make it inaccessible to the
many and uninteresting to most of us.

Worse, in their zeal for pursuing the "facts," they have
led us further away than ever from the unraveling of our
essential mystery: What is it that makes our sexuality possible? How do we go about finding it? And how can we
keep it alive?

This book is an attempt to deal with these and other
basic questions of the nature of human sexuality. Strictly
speaking, it is only incidentally about sex. I am concerned
with the issues of boundaries, the borders of our outer and
inner selves. Those limits are developed in the sexuality
of the experience we call childhood. And they are maintained and constantly tested, stretched and occasionally
breached, in the sexual lives we live as adults.

Sexuality happens at those boundaries. Sexuality creates
the boundaries in the first place, shapes them, develops
them, and is, in turn, transformed by them through its
successive possibilities of joy and despair. It is through our
experience of our boundaries that our sexuality becomes
what it is: the means of reaching the greatest pleasure we
can know in life, the vehicle for establishing the closest
links, the greatest joy between the separate strangers we are.
And the easiest means for debasing, destroying, defiling the
precious accident that is life itself.

The question that emerges from this is the one that has
often given the spur to novelists and poets: Why is it that
sexual loving is at once so powerful and yet so fragile?

In answer, I have not designed an elaborate laboratory

methodology, nor have I chosen to quote from the large number of authorities whose work impinges on mine. Instead, I have given credit to those whose ideas have most influenced my own. Largely, my theory is derived from my own experience in living and from sharing with my patients in their own hard-won struggles for insight. Some of their experiences appear, in disguised form, in this book, a fragment from one person's life along with a piece of living from another's, to make up the people I have invented as examples.

What I do have to offer, instead of statistics and authorities, is an original theory of sexuality that will be unacceptable to some, controversial to many. I believe it can offer a powerful way to make sense out of chaos.

I have been witness to that chaos and to its destructive potential from the beginnings of my work with families, as a resident psychiatrist in training at Harvard (Massachusetts Mental Health Center). Its continued presence has informed my professional experience of nearly fifteen years as family therapist and as teacher and supervisor of other professionals-in-training at Boston's three medical schools, Harvard, Tufts, and Boston University. Increasingly, as my practice has shifted to focus on the many difficulties inherent in the varieties of human sexual expression, and as my patients, as individuals, as couples, as families, have struggled with me to find help, some new insights have come which may be of use to any healthy growing person.

This is not a book about sexual technique. What you may learn is a way of looking at your sexuality that can give new life to every position you know already—especially the erect and vertical one of normal everyday living.

And though I hope through these insights to enrich the

sexual lives of adults, it is ultimately the kids I am after.

For if we have gained in sexual freedom in any tangible way, it is surely in the freedom to discuss sex openly. Only, as I said before, we don't know how to go about doing it.

Yes, we can teach the facts of life to our kids.

But what facts?

Do we want them to know the technicalities of sexual connection? Yes. Certainly that. To dispel ignorance and fear and to prevent cruelty and pain, they must be given those facts. But a cold technology is not only amoral but really not much more useful than the mythology it supersedes; in some instances, where the myth supports a spirit of adventure and fosters hope, the sterile knowledge of technique is worse.

No. Technique, mere instruction in the coupling of the genitals and all the "facts," may be useful but it is not enough. If we would be truly helpful and loving as parents and teachers, we must show the kids that sex is not merely what goes on in bed. And that it involves more than the experience of beauty and pleasure; we must somehow tell the truth about its difficulties, not as clinical exceptions but as common realities. We need to show the pain as well as the pleasure, the ugly and the beautiful, to help them to transcend both and really begin to live their sexual lives.

JAY KUTEN, M.D.

Tinakilly House, County Wicklow, Ireland
and Nashumah, Henniker, New Hampshire

1

Happily-Ever-Aftering

BOY MEETS GIRL. Boy chases girl. Boy gets girl. And they live happily ever after. Recognize those words? That plot? Of course. We've heard the story so often in its thousands of variations since the fairy tales of our childhood. We've had it served with cookies and milk or over popcorn in movie after movie until it's become a part of our dreams, part of all of our expectations for ourselves. For we live out lives whose measure cannot fail to be taken from the shared dreams of our culture—its mythology.

And what happens when our lives don't measure up? We want to meet someone, someone beautiful and good and true. To love them and have them love us. Happily ever after. And what happens to us when we find out it's not so easy as our myths allow? That meetings are full of terror and anguish. That loving is full of fear and anger. That there may be no true happy-ever-after, but only successive partings and their sorrow. When even sex, which is so valued by us, which is to hold it all together, comes apart, even forces us apart. Is our choice, then, between despair at disappointment, between the rage of frustrated hope, and a new try at the golden ring on the same merry-go-round? Or is there something else? Something we can learn by knowing ourselves a little better? By knowing more about the sexual loving we seek as adults, how it comes to be what it is, how it falters and fails, maybe even what it needs to keep it going.

After all, when we've heard all the love stories and played the parts in our heads time after time, we have to ask, "Why not for me?" We are the beautiful princess and we are the handsome prince. We expect to fall in love and to marry and to live happily ever after.

Only we don't. Perhaps it's because we're not beautiful enough. Not handsome enough. Or maybe—just maybe—it's because that story has always ended too soon. And ours goes on.

Lucille is in her twenties, bright, blonde, and beautiful. And she is terrified of men. It's not that she doesn't like them, of course. Far from it. She does. She would like to find one and maybe even marry someday. Settle down and have kids. But every time she is so much as introduced to a man, she is so frightened that the hair on her neck stands up and she backs away, almost on the verge of spitting. When she does go out with a man, the evening is full of hidden threat and almost certain to end in some frustrating outburst of anger. It's the only way she knows, for now, to keep a man from overwhelming her. In her teens her mother used to accuse her of all sorts of sexual license and call her a slut. Now, grown older, she feels a little out of control when a man makes a pass at her or even when he pays her the slightest attention. She is afraid of her feelings and of his anger. If somehow a man penetrates her rather formidable defenses and manages to kiss her, she will almost certainly go to bed with him, feeling no pleasure in it, almost unconscious. Her one steady in the last year is a fellow who has a serious physical deformity. Somehow she feels a little safer with him because she feels her superiority. But it's not enough for her to go out with a man she doesn't really admire, and purely for the physical convenience. She sees life slipping by, a succession of little miseries with no immediate hope for relief. So she is sitting crying quietly in my office, tears trailing down the corners of her eyes, over her freckled cheeks.

Madeleine is a talented musician. She's been living with Jeffrey for nine months now. It is two years since her divorce from Robert became final. She and Robert were married when still in high school. Five years later they realized they had been too young. Now, in her mid twenties, she is more cautious. She would like to see how things work out a little before making any extensive commitment. Besides, Jeffrey is an artist and neither of them have any serious hope of earning a decent living for quite a while. Their arrangement seems to be working out for both of them, but every now and again Madeleine gets depressed, usually around the time of her period. She also finds herself flying into sudden and inexplicable rages. Like three nights ago.

"A friend of Jeff's came over. Like he just dropped in from L.A. and I had no idea he would want to stay over. But he did. Before that, though, we all were just sitting around rapping after dinner. Then I started to clean up and Jeff and Don went into the front room to smoke and talk.

Suddenly I began to feel a little strange. Alone. Very distant from the two of them. Like I couldn't reach them, especially Jeff. And I began to feel cold and to shiver. So I went to bed. Later, when Jeff came in, he told me Don was staying over. I just rolled over and I couldn't have anything to do with him. I had this terrific headache that lasted practically the whole next day. It didn't go away until Don did. The funny thing is that I like Don. I mean, he's a nice person. Only somehow I know I was angry that he was there. I couldn't tell Jeffrey, though. He's always into a big rap about sharing and open house and all that. I couldn't tell him anyway. When I get angry I just seem to curl up inside myself, like into a round ball."

Werner and Clarice have been married for just under two years. Werner, about ten years older than his wife, is a sophisticated and charming man from a European family. Clarice came from a little New England town and spent her early years with nuns. She fell for him like the proverbial ton of bricks. They have been pretty happy. Except. . . . A few months after their marriage Clarice suddenly began to feel that she was not intelligent enough for Werner's old friends. And she felt Werner shared their view. She became intensely suspicious of him when he was away on business and thought seriously of having him followed. The feelings diminished somewhat over the months. Yet even today, if Werner should look overlong at an attractive woman Clarice has twinges and, later, a tantrum. And Werner has always had an eye for the ladies.

Carl and Betty consulted me for help with a sexual problem. Their marriage of ten years had been a fairly good

4

one, they felt, except in the sex department. It had never been particularly great. Both had been virgins when they married, and Carl had been too shy to date anyone except Betty. Betty had had some other involvements and sexual experience short of intercourse. Carl had always resented his wife's experience and occasionally threw it up to her in the few minor arguments they had. They argued very seldom, preferring instead to try to reason things out. However, this sexual problem wouldn't respond to reason. And since the birth of their child, there had been less and less sex. And no apparent reason. Things were calm between them, smooth on the surface. Carl had been very busy building a law practice, and Betty tried to keep occupied by taking courses at the university to finish the requirements for her degree. They had thought of affairs as a way of resolution, but neither really wanted to follow that path. So they had come for help instead.

Frank and Sally, both in their fifties, were at the tail end of their relationship. Theirs had been a short, tempestuous marriage which followed upon a long and torrid love affair. Things seemed to go downhill almost from the moment it became legal.

Frank: "Christ, I don't know what the hell to do. So help me, I'm afraid I'm gonna kill her. She just keeps following me around. Never lets up. Never lets me alone. I feel choked. She wants to know what I'm doing all the time. I don't know. I tell you I don't know what the hell to do."

Sally: "He's lying. I mean, this is not the same sweet man I married. He's always pushing me away. When I go to touch him or make any move toward him, he acts like I'm poison. And believe me, I've never had to chase after a man before. I don't know what's the matter with him. Or with me."

On this particular occasion they are describing the details of a fight they had that began with an apparently lighthearted joke in which Frank called her mother an "old gasbag" and that ended with stitches taken in both their hides at the local hospital. As they described and chewed over the weary details of who said what to whom, first and last, they re-created the atmosphere of their home, where each tried to corner the other and prove him "wrong."

What do all these people have in common? With each other—and with us? For one thing, they're all dealing with love and sexuality, with wishes for good things and with hurt and disappointment when good things go wrong. And each is dealing in his own way with the problem of demarcating the boundaries of his emotional space.

The problems of sex and of loving have been described before in a variety of contexts, but the relationship of these two parts of human experience to the development and the continued maintenance of a person's boundaries, of the borders of his selfhood—that has not yet been adequately explored. And exploring it offers a powerful way of understanding the difficulties involved in sexual loving, a way of shedding light on the mysteries of human interaction.

Let's look again at Lucille. She has to work damn hard to remain as she is. After all, an attractive girl gets many opportunities to meet men. Yet one of her complaints is that she never meets them. If you ask her how that can be, she'll admit softly that when she does meet a man and he appears interesting and she is interested, she does her damnedest to make sure he loses interest fast—through some bit of sarcasm, some tactlessness. Or she can say, "I don't know what to say to a man." Never mind that her therapist is male and she is talking (albeit with difficulty). She does *know what to say*. And it is usually in the form of a hostile comment. So she asks, "What do men want? I don't know what men want!"

You have to ask why this good-looking, healthy, intelligent girl works so hard to keep from getting snapped up by an equally good-looking, healthy, intelligent guy, right? Asking *why* will get somewhere, of course. After a long time and after her life history is spread out like a battle map or a flayed skin, the origins of her conflicts will possibly be clearer. And then where are you? Probably back at the beginning to get *her* to see it and maybe to change. But if you ask *how*, then things might go differently. How does she do it so consistently and so well? After all, warding off the temptation of all potentially rewarding relationships takes energy. It takes a great deal of energy just to maintain one's rationalizations that this one is a bastard, and the other one is worthless, and that one is just interested in sex, and that one . . . It takes strength and energy to maintain one's preconceived notions. But the expense is worth it if the alternative is to feel the painful anxiety of openness, of vulnerability to intrusion by another.

Why intrusion? Why should meeting an attractive person, engaging with that person, and maybe getting romantically involved with him be anything at all like an intrusion, the forced entry of a frightening or, in any case, an unwanted stranger? Because that, in fact, is what they are. Strangers. And to become acquaintances, friends, intimates, lovers, they must pass through successive layers of her personal boundaries, the protective roadblocks surrounding her inner self.

Lucille, maybe a little more than most people, is acutely aware of the *strangeness* of these strangers, the men who might like to meet her, get to know her, do God knows what else to her. To her, in the labyrinth of her experiences, these men pose more of a threat than they do to others; they mean something to her that is uniquely personal and uniquely threatening. So she rejects them in advance. Never lets them past the first hello.

She differs from most of us in the intensity of her fear and in the special meaning she attaches to what she is afraid of. But her style differs not in kind but only in degree from our own. For we all operate at some level of awareness of threat when we meet some new person, and the more so when that person is someone in whom we have an interest, someone who could touch us, someone who could have some meaning for us, someone who could get past our guard.

Well, what about the fact that Lucille is involved with a man, whom she sees sporadically but sees nevertheless? A man with whom she has sexual relations. That's getting past somebody's guard, isn't it? A girl who's so uptight that meeting a fellow and talking pleasantly is a major calamity —how is she able, with the same set of prejudices and problems, to bed down with anyone at all? Contradiction? Paradox? Not exactly. Just another way of expressing and experiencing the same anxiety. Only backwards, this time.

As much as she fears the threat of new meetings, she finds unbearable the experience of parting and losing. Men, whatever they mean to her, are threatening to that part of her which is inside, vulnerable behind those apparently formidable defenses. What will they do to that intimate part if allowed access, in freedom? Perhaps the worst is that they will not want the gift. That they will leave and offer that wounded core another proof that there really *is* something to fear out there. By committing herself sexually to a man she doesn't really care about she has a little insurance. Or, by making sure, with any man she finds herself sexually responsive, that she does *not* care, not about him, not about the sex, she protects herself from the pain of future parting. By going about the business of encounter and involvement this way with men she devalues, Lucille is spared the insult of their good-byes. After all, rejection is nothing much if it comes from someone you don't really care about. By avoiding men she *could* care for, she attempts to spare herself the threat of their hello.

There is no contradiction for her or anyone else who must operate in this way. And to a degree that means all of us. Because both kinds of maneuvers are geared to dealing with a similar kind of anxiety. An anxiety that exists at the boundaries of a person's intimate space. To have someone leave that space and pass that boundary, or to come in through it, elicits special feelings of vulnerability. We all have that vulnerability in common; yet its meaning is made unique by each one's personal history. We all share with Lucille that predisposition to anxiety, our own unique form of anxiety, at the threat of having to open ourselves up, whether it is to let someone part from us or to take someone in.

These feelings of anxiety, of terror even, are generated at the surface of encounter, at the time of *getting together*. In an important way, these first few moments are a microcosm of the relationship that may follow, a sort of capsule version of what will be established when and if the couple get together at *making it happen*; and further, a good basis for predicting how they may go about the business of *letting go*, then, later, and, if need be, finally. Small wonder there's a lot riding on those first few moments.

It's a truism among clinicians in the mental-health field that the first five minutes of an interview reveal everything and contain everything. All the defenses, all the secrets, all the elements of a person's little hidden traits, are laid bare to scrutiny. That afterward the therapy that may go on for months and even for years is all downhill. Perhaps there is some exaggeration in this notion, but the immediate part of any first meeting does contain the most-defended and the least-defended elements of a person's being. And it's all one, all a transparent struggle. If the notion has validity, it is because in those first few moments of encounter the anxiety which people experience at the prospect of loosening their defensive boundaries forces them to struggle with themselves briefly. In that struggle, instead of revealing less, they reveal more of themselves than they intended. Perhaps it can be said that for a moment they have gone slightly mad.

Interpreting the subtle cues of that special instant of insanity has become the province of some very innovative men, from Wilhem Reich, who launched the study of character analysis in modern psychiatry with his consideration of the body as character armor, to the people at Esalen Institute in California, who are trying to teach others the language of their bodies. Because the anxiety of encounter is not rational, it cannot be easily wafted away with the measured words of academic discourse or the straight talk of the marketplace. It is the speech of the body, and the first and best place it can be understood is in the body.

We meet someone and there is suddenly a moment of fear and trembling, a tension that holds on and that is mutual. The spark of that anxiety passes between the two of us and we are both caught up in it. Suddenly, the heart rate increases, and the breathing deepens and slows, the eyes dilate and the mouth dries a bit. The muscles congest with blood. Inwardly, there is that quivery feeling, that quickening in the gut that we commonly associate with danger, with the possibility of attack. Here we are, two healthy, attractive strangers trying to make contact, and it's like preparing for a kind of primitive combat. Here we are just getting to know each other, *finding out*, and it's like we're ready to tear each other apart.

Maybe there *is* something primitive going on. After all, ethologists, on the basis of their work with animals other than man, have given us observations of the threatening stances that animals assume when they meet as strangers. It makes no difference, at first, that the other animal is of a different sex, that he or she is a potential sex partner. It is simply a stranger, though of the same species. The first concern is the aggressive one of establishing one's boundaries, the right of dominion over a specific territory, the authority over food and favor of a given region. Once that territoriality is established and the boundaries are respected and everyone "knows" just what's what and who's who, the possibility of sex can be entertained. The conversion from a possible struggle to the death to a peaceful moment of recognition requires that rituals of transformation be devised, rituals that incorporate the gestures of aggression and of acquiescence. A kind of ritual combat. Konrad Lorenz emphasizes in his book *On Aggression* that the outward signs of "anger" (if such it can be called in these animals) appear to be greater in this kind of struggle, one between equals, than, say, in the struggle between predator and prey.

In recent years there have been a number of extrapolations from the study of animal behavior to inferences about the meaning of human behavior. Most popular has been the work of Desmond Morris, whose book *The Naked Ape* is replete with illustrations of our close tie to our animal forbears as seen in the complex rituals and behaviors of daily existence. For example, smiling is, according to this view, a part of a complex interaction ritual in which we overcome our own inner anxiety and the anxiety of those whom we smile upon—and do not devour. We shake hands and in so doing assure each other that our palms are open, and unprepared with weapon or with fist for combat. Or we may share food, ritually (and less for nourishment), or a mild intoxicant, alcohol or tobacco, or marijuana, signaling that our purpose is not to eat one another, but to share ceremonially instead, and, in so doing, to form a tie and a relationship. Perhaps, then, it's just a pure invention when we imagine, meeting someone new, that he is about to open his mouth and gobble us up, or perhaps a dim memory from a primordial past. But how can the primitive animal nervous system which inhabits the bodies of all of us really know for sure that it's O.K., that we are safe after all. Anyway, we can reach for another drink. An intuitive grasp of the profit to be made and the reason for it must have inspired the first fellow who converted his neighborhood saloon, where the regulars gathered and drank, slowly, lovingly, into a dating bar, where the action is, and the liquor flows like weak tea.

Yes, we want to meet and explore this other person, but

there is fear, too, and a need for some means to get over it. It is not just the threat of the other person in his newness that we feel; it is the sense of our own vulnerability, the weakness of our boundaries, and the portent of anxiety which we will experience in relaxing those boundaries.

The degree of anxiety, the intensity of fear, is a reflection of our own felt need. The most frightened people are those who most need the closeness, who most desperately yearn to let someone in. They know somewhere how badly they want someone. And, knowing that need, fear even more the helplessness of letting go, even slightly, of themselves, and of the other, lest all their defenses, *all* their boundaries, vanish. A common response then is to raise the barrier even higher, as Lucille does, to deflect any possibility that someone will enter our emotional space. Or to use artificial means, some alcohol or pot, or an elaborate ritual, to erase from our awareness the knowledge that the barriers even exist.

Well, if it's all this much trouble just to get started, how the devil do people ever manage? How do they fall in love, marry, stay married? How do they even keep alive? Especially if our patterns of courtship are only a slight step away from those of the lower animals, from, say, the ghastly cannibalism of the praying mantis, which actually devours its mate during sexual relations. No wonder there's anxiety. No wonder there's distrust. But what about love? What about sexual attraction? Don't these rather powerful forces exert an influence? People do seem to get over the hurdle of first meetings, of blind dates, and they've even managed to perpetuate their kind, following the old Biblical injunction to be fruitful and multiply, in so strong a way as to endanger the planet.

Yes, of course, they manage. But not without pain. And

after the meetings and the pairings there are the long days and nights of loving, but with the pain of hatred, and still, if their relationship is sexual and remains so, the fear continues to exist, the anxiety remains.

Lucille's fear is one thing, this stranger anxiety. Perhaps it can be dismissed as a useless remnant of primordial days, like an appendix, something that once was necessary and now exists on its own, without value, but still a source of trouble. But what about the others, the countless others who have gotten over that first hurdle, who have committed themselves to loving in some measure, like the people introduced at the beginning of this chapter?

Can it be that love is not enough? That sex is not the answer we've been led to believe? It runs against our grain, our expectations of anything from ecstasy to quiet happiness, of "happily-ever-aftering." Instead there are the lonely nights, angry dawns. There is love. There is sex. But there is still anxiety. And hatred. And they are almost inextricably interwoven in adult life. When we're all grown up it's hard to see how loving gives over so easily to its opposite. We have to look at the beginnings. Only a look, a long look at how sexuality and loving develop in human growth within the human family will make it possible for us to unravel things. And we will need to trace that central thread, that anxiety, which persists uncomfortably within the fabric of relationships, tying together the apparent contradictions of feeling and motivation, of sex and aggression, of love and hatred.

Remember that adults don't just invent sexuality.

The teacher had just finished giving her first-graders the basic facts of life. Little Mary raised her hand from a front-

14

row seat. "Can a six-year-old boy make a baby?" "No," said the teacher, smiling, "that would be impossible. Any other questions, class?" Pause. Mary again put her hand up. "Can a six-year-old girl make a baby?" "No," said the teacher. Whereupon the little boy behind Mary leaned forward and whispered loudly in her ear, "Ya see! I told ya, ya didn't have nothin' to worry about!"

Sexuality grows from the first moments of life, from the earliest bases of personal involvement. From the body. Along with other complex functions, it exists in its primitive form at the moment of birth. The newborn gasps, sucks hungrily to fill its lungs with precious air, and then it cries, sending the air out again over tiny vocal cords. Later that simple noise, that cry transformed by time and growth and experience, will become speech and language. His diminutive arms extend and then pump inward toward his chest, and his hands clench into a fist the size of a golf ball. One day those hands which are now so crudely helpless may play a Mozart sonata or be clenched around a tennis racket and may, along with more developed arms, be capable of throwing a baseball ninety miles an hour. Or the legs that are today fit for a little more than thrashing wildly may someday carry him to victory in a marathon or simply from his car to a seat in front of the television. And sexuality? It begins as the pleasurable activity of all parts of the body, its surface of skin and even softer tissue and its inner parts, the organ systems. It *is* the sum total of the body's pleasure. It includes the pleasure derived from apperception of all the senses, of touching, of seeing, of smelling; it includes the proprioception of muscular activity. Pleasure from all the perceived activities of the internal organs is a part of it—pleasure derived from the functioning of the digestive tract and its peristaltic motion, the contractile waves along the gut from mouth to anus, pleasure from the circulatory and respiratory systems, the beating of the heart, the experiencing of vessels in vasodilatation and constriction, the rhythmic breathing, out and in, pleasure from the urinary tract and from the genitals, capable even early in life of congestion, of tumescence. And most importantly, the working of the central nervous system, the crude computer of a brain revving up, the peripheral nerves in touch with the world.

The basis for the idea that pleasure derived from the whole of bodily activity constitutes the sexual life of infants is the work of Sigmund Freud. Today, we live in a post-Freudian universe, a world so much influenced by his work that we tend to take it for granted because it seems as if we have always known these things or as if they were inherently obvious. But it's not at all that obvious that infants have a sexual life. Certainly if you get confused over the words "sexual life" and only images of copulating adults come to mind, superimposed upon the tiny bodies of children, you may find yourself repelled by the idea, but you will not have understood the concept or its implications.

And it is *not* intuitively obvious that the sexuality of infancy ought to be the pleasure of the total body. Freud postulated that infantile sexuality *was* equivalent to the pleasurable activity of the body in order to provide a means for understanding the mature sexual functioning of adults, and how it came to be. He realized that adult sexuality must originate in the experiences of earliest childhood. By equating the pleasures derived from all the life-sustaining activities of the body, he arrived at a great jumping-off point for exploration of the growth of sexual pleasure. But it entails the proposition that the sexuality of adults represents a narrowing, a shrinkage from the sexuality of infants. Originally, sexuality includes *all* the delight experienced in the active life of *all* the body. In becoming an adult, the pattern of sexuality which emerges from the infant's wide capacity for pleasure has been narrowed in range and concentrated mainly on one organ system, the genitals.

Now, that idea seems unflattering to us at first, so accustomed are we adults to thinking of ourselves as specially favored by divine generosity. After all, we know our adult experience from the inside. We know it's a pretty good thing (give or take a little bit), and the notion that it's only a part of what is possible for a little kid not only seems farfetched and somewhat demeaning but doesn't jibe with the facts of our remembered childhood. We know that our sexual behavior, like most other adult functioning, is learned, that it has undergone a process of education (in this case, largely of self-education) from the earliest fumbling moments of embarrassed unfastenings to our present suave assurance. (Oh, well, anyway, a quick drink and you hardly feel a bit nervous.) We see the history of our development and we know that we know *now* more than we did *then*. Kids? What have they got? A few games of house? A few sessions of play-doctor?

The insult is only imagined, not real. One thing that stands in the way of acceptance of infantile sexuality as a powerful conceptual tool for understanding ourselves as adults is that we confuse the process of development with that which undergoes development. Yes, growth, experience, time, learning, increase the complexity and richness of sexuality and shape it to its adult form. But the developing sexuality of infants has a richness too, the vast richness of total potential.

This way of looking at adult sexuality as growing from infantile sexuality, implicitly by a process of selection, of pruning, of increasing differentiation, brings sexuality in line with other complex facets of man's evolution in culture.

Take language.

Children are born with a fantastic richness of potential and actual soundings. They make all kinds of noises to themselves or others as soon as they are able. They have the potential for developing any and all of the sound patternings that go into making up any and all of the languages of man. Pluck up that city-born white middle-class baby and set him down and raise him in South Africa and he will easily acquire Xhosa with its sparkling palate-snapping click sounds. Put him in Peking and he'll speak Chinese. But leave him where he is, at home with you, and he will learn English (or American, or whatever common tongue we all share that divides us) and he will gradually lose that wonderful potential in the process of his selection of *our* sound patterns, until the point where, in the tenth grade, learning German, a cousin to our own language, will prove quite a hurdle. And French. Well, sooner see the French kids learn English. Once the choice of language is made (by plunking the child down in one country), he goes on to learn that language, to refine it, to master it. A selection process occurs, and then a differentiation process, learning, follows. And in the process of learning, of differentiating and developing the selected phonemic patterns, the original total potential is partly given up, the original capacity for speaking in any tongue is partly lost, forgotten though not necessarily irretrievably.

Language is easily the most obvious function that is modified in individual and cultural evolution. And, of course, is still in active evolution in the life of each individual. We could look at other functions to see their evolutionary development, such as the skilled use of appendages in their elaboration through tools and to the elaboration of new tools; or at complex patterns of socialization, modified as we know them to be by so many levels of influence, the individual, himself, his family, the culture.

But sexuality is something special. Because it includes all the rest, in the special way in which Freud defined its origins, and we have defined it here, as the infantile delight in the pleasurable activity of all parts of the human body. And because it is so *inclusive,* the concept of infantile sexuality lets us trace not only the development of sexuality as an experience of the body but the complex feelings of love and hate and anxiety that come along the way.

This process of sexual development happens within the human family.

Human development is unique in that it takes so long from infancy to maturity. Other mammals have made use of a family structure for social living. And birds. And insects have complex communities. But no other animal spends so much of his life span with a family structure, just growing up, dependent.

During that prolonged dependency, the child is protected in one way or another from the harsh demands of reality and economic necessity. Those early years, especially, are a period of privileged irresponsibility. And more particularly in our culture. The more industrialized and affluent the society, the longer the period of dependence, the greater the degree of protection and consequently of irresponsibility. Conversely, where there is general poverty and all must work to survive, even the small children are called upon to perform tasks that are needed by the family and consequently they early assume legitimized roles and in turn become defined by them.

Our society seems until most recently to have needed its children less and less for any serious immediate purpose. It's altogether like the somewhat tasteless joke about the very rich lady whose chauffeur was pushing her handsome, healthy-looking, grown-up son about in a wheel chair. As she passed down the avenue another woman looked at the strapping lad and remarked to her friend what a pity it was that such a fine-looking young man couldn't walk. Whereupon the rich mother spun on her with "Oh, he can walk all right. But, thank God. He doesn't have to!"

This irresponsibility that is built into our family life promotes a blossoming of desires and sets the stage for disappointment.

To understand best how this works in the development of sexuality, it's necessary to try to crunch up your viewpoint, to get on all fours and try to look at the world from the position of an infant. Early in life, the world is a pretty funny place. One important feature which it lacks is boundaries. To a newborn child, there is no clear-cut beginning and ending of himself. In time or in space. There *is* no time or space. He is the world and the world is him. There is no "inside" and no "outside"; everything is all together and "is" the baby. The process of splitting things off, of deciding that there is a world out there and it's not you, of building boundaries between yourself and others, between what is "inside" and what is "outside" you, these are all parts of human history, parts of the lifelong process of becoming an individual.

But before all that, this baby, whose viewpoint we have borrowed, is living a life which is vastly sensual. He is totally surrounded, bombarded, by sensual stimuli. He is grooving on his whole body. He is also accepting the whole world as a part of his domain. And so the world becomes a pretty sexual place, especially as it provides a means for the infant to be satisfied, for the child to be delighted in his body.

Of all the possible influences in the world, there is one relationship which stands above all the others in importance, the tie between the child and its mother. Now we know that a child's mother is actually responsible for much that is pleasure in his life, for satisfying elemental needs, for keeping him alive. In many ways it's fair to say she *is* his world. She is the source of life and the provider of the means to sustain it. (Just see how quickly we revert to form on that other perilous journey into outer life. We talk about "life-support systems" in the astronaut's techno-jargon, and the spacecraft soon becomes the "mother ship.") The mother takes care of the child's body in countless ways, great and small, becoming the source of most of the pleasure in existence. The baby does little, at first, to provide for his own amusement. But it is finally his to register. It is through his senses, of his own body, through his brain, which receives the impressions and records and assimilates and judges them, that the child "knows" he is having pleasure. But what he does not know is that there is an external source of his pleasure. What *he* experiences is a global, diffuse sense, somehow perceived as "good," all over his universe as far as he can comprehend it. These blurry shapes of grandparents, strangers, sisters, brothers, even that of a fairly constant one with the wonderful smell, the delicious taste, the good feeling of warmth, even that *one* shape doesn't make meaningful sense to him, *at first*, and so is passed on by the fledgling computer-brain that is starting to learn to scan and interpret. All he knows is the perception of momentary discomfort, of wetness, or cold, or hunger, all in great magnitude, but dim of form and without shape—there is no way, yet, of classifying this or that unpleasure as cold, or as wet, or as hunger. It's all unpleasure until learning makes it possible to unscramble—it's all unpleasure until he makes some effort to relieve the pain and bring the pleasure back. He moves, thrashes, then makes his face into a grimace, constricts his throat to force out air, and cries. And suddenly, it's better. The world is its old familiar shape again. Life is pleasure again. The good smell, the good taste, the good warmth, are back again, the inner feeling of goodness—and all of it, mother, or because of mother, but there is no word for it yet. No mommy. No mama. There is not even the idea of a separate thing to be recognized as mother. There is only the child's world, the sexually pleasurable world of his body. And everything is in it as far as his mind can reach.

That is the child's position and it is also his problem. Sensory experience, dimly understood, constitutes a universe of pleasure and unpleasure. The pleasure is the delight derived from the activities of the body, a body which, as yet, knows no boundaries, and the pursuit of it *is* the sexual activity of the child. But the pleasure which the child perceives as his own must arise from what happens between himself and the mother who assumes such total care for him *and* his body. Only, for a long time, he is unable to recognize that she is not simply part of him. (It's *his* world, you see. It's *his* pleasure.)

But failure to recognize his separateness leaves the child peculiarly vulnerable to the effects of a paradox that will haunt his entire life of loving.

On the one hand, he is powerless and totally dependent upon mother, for his very life. On the other, the failure to see mother's separate existence leads to a false feeling of omnipotence, a belief in the ability to secure total indulgence in pleasure free from any restraint or limitation.

There is a cartoon that brilliantly spotlights this peculiar perspective. Two laboratory mice are talking inside an experimental cage. One reassures the other: "Look, there's nothing to worry about here. I've got this big guy trained. Every time I press this bar he drops in a hunk of food."

It is in coming to terms with our omnipotent wishes and with the actualities of our limitations, our continued relative helplessness, that wisdom is attained. In truth, we never fully succeed. We continue to struggle to fulfill those early wishes for total indulgence. It is this struggle which has led more than one serious observer of humankind to remark that Linnaeus was a bit premature in classifying us as *Homo sapiens*. Our sapience is still a distant goal for the species and the individual man. No matter. Whether we actively seek wisdom, prefer the longing of infancy, or succumb to the pressures of existence, the cost is high in any case.

The cost of the struggle is the pain of anxiety.

The confrontation of his weakness, his impotence with respect to external, objective reality as against his wished-for and believed-in omnipotence, brings the child to his first experience with the painful inner state of turmoil that he will later learn to call *anxiety*. He believes that he is everything and everywhere and that the good feelings he experiences are really at his summons and control. He can have everything he wants, since what he wants is to continue feeling good. Somewhere, of course, mother, who is the source of all his pleasure (or, at the least, is the basis upon which that pleasure can happen), must betray his world to her own. Sometime, in her simple good-willed humanity, she must do those things which mark her own individuality, even if it's only to forget to change him for too long a time, or to skip his feeding because her own life must take priority for the moment. Then, suddenly, he is confronted with unpleasure that won't go away at his wish or his cry. Maybe she returns, doesn't disappoint him totally, the first time. Perhaps it will require several repetitions until he suddenly is trapped by the reality of his helplessness. And in terms he cannot ignore. For it must set off all the body's basic alarm systems, the autonomic discharge, the rush of adrenalin running the heart, giving surges of power to the muscles, clenching down the intestine. The body is alerted, prepared, even if there is no way it can be prepared in such a helpless state—for danger. Such a shock is a threat to life, his total life as he has known it. It is the feeling of impending annihilation.

That is how he becomes aware of his separateness. And as threatening to life as that experience of anxiety appears, this naturally developing conflict of opposing realities, the inner one of the child and the outer one of the world, is the basis upon which learning and growth take place. It is the way through which his own individuality develops, the means whereby the structure of his selfhood unfolds. And the vulnerability that tests and shapes his capacity for forming enduring human relationships, in the atmosphere of trust necessary to do so. Finally, it's a kind of hell-fire that he must momentarily but repeatedly endure in order to be able to give in love as well as to receive.

If anxiety signals to the child this important living conflict, when does it begin? We could all easily agree that the inherent discrepancy, and hence the conflict, between a wish for omnipotence and a reality of limitation and relative impotence, is with us all our lives. In a sense one could regard the achievements of *Homo faber*, technological man, as part of a game that he must play to keep out of awareness the fact of his mortality, that most essential helplessness. It is not so difficult to show, once the concept is granted, that all the engines of culture are fired partly by the energy which man generates as he tries to resolve the conflict. Yet for an individual human it is hard to pin down the moment the struggle begins and the state of anxiety develops.

But given the experience that it is, the shock, the mobilizing alarm system that touches all of the body in its effect, we can look for the *physiologic* basis for experiencing that helplessness with the first moments of life. The massive shock to the body's systems of having to sustain life independently, feeding itself the essential nutriments in its own circulatory system, supplying its own energy for metabolism in breathing, providing for its own excretion of waste—that shift from physical attachment to mother and dependence upon *her* body's functions to comparative independence is never matched in magnitude throughout life by any other change, except perhaps death itself. That change—birth—with its attendant physical responses and adaptations, serves as a model. All the physical events later defined as anxiety happen to an even greater degree at birth. And anxiety which is experienced later will be referred back in some recess of memory to those first uncertain moments of independent life, if only because the moment of total extinction, the possibility of annihilation, is certainly present at birth. What we *experience* as anxiety are the bodily concomitants of that struggle; we *interpret* that experience as a sense of the threat of annihilation. Our ability to make that interpretation, to interpret anxiety as a threat to life, is what distinguishes us from other animals, who also struggle but presumably do not see the ultimate outcome of the struggle. Hence they, unlike us, have no need to explain themselves, and no need to try to make over reality.

For humans, these events which remind us of our weakness, our separateness, the fact that death is close at hand, must generate the bodily experience of anxiety. Birth is the first moment of true *physical* separation. Those complex physical rearrangements are nearly matched in intricacy by the subtleties of the process of *emotional* separation. The comprehension of it is the slow process of a lifetime struggle. It is a struggle which centers around love and the threat of the loss of that love in becoming separated from that *which is loved*. That threat produces anxiety in the child's body. And that inner bodily state of discomfort is referred back to its basis in the child's own life history of experience of separations already endured, the first and most disruptive being birth. And every time he must endure, throughout life, the threat of separation and loss of love, he will suffer that anxiety, just as if it were all happening again, for the first time, the gasping for new air in the struggle against extinction.

If anxiety has its physiologic basis in birth, and arises later in response to the threat of new separations, in response to the loss of love, how does love itself enter the

26

picture? Love is at the opposite position. Love is first of all the relation of the ego, the inner organizing principle of experience, to the sources of pleasure. Love begins with the satisfaction of needs because that *is* the pleasure of the child. And since the satisfaction of needs is seen to come from oneself, in a world that is all *him*, the earliest love is the love of self through bodily satisfaction. It is, we know, mother who makes this possible; by providing consistent means of satisfying the child's needs, she makes it possible for the child to love himself. And to continue to do so, in the fragile manner of infancy.

Since the child sees mother as part of his universe, the loving feelings are extended to her, to the vague shape and scent and warmth that are all she can be to him at first. Love begins, then, as a measure of self-sufficiency, well-being, a feeling of general "good," extending itself to the mother as an external representation of the good feelings of satisfaction which the child already has inside. This is very important, because love, in this view, is based not on denial of self but on affirmation of self. To love at all, one must first love the self. In later life one will need to love others not because of insufficiency, or mental illness, but to *prevent* oneself from becoming ill through having no one to love *but* oneself. Love, seen this way, is the means of extending one's boundaries. And just as the earliest loved one is seen as part of oneself, which is somehow external, later loved ones will be easily internalized, incorporated into the self.

The first love, then, is the love of the self, the child's love of his own body as the source of pleasure. The earliest love is the love of oneself as a sexual being, as a body generating pleasure in its activity. And if love is what the child feels toward the sources of pleasures, and sexuality is pleasure derived from the active life of the entire body, it follows that, in the beginning of life, love *is* the feeling of infantile sexuality. And, as *feeling*, love is a part of the body's pleasurable activity. Hence, love and sexuality are well-nigh indistinguishable in the infant. And love is the sexual relationship of the infant self to the body.

That sexual loving is extended to mother in the mistaken notion that she is a part of that body. Parenthetically, it is a crucial step in development for the child to love mother as a thing apart from himself, a separate being. It implies that the child has experienced the sense of being separate long enough for its reality to impress him, and that he has not only survived but somehow grown in the process. He has had to let mother go, out of his boundaries and out of his immediate emotional space, while retaining not only his good feelings for himself but those for her as well. As we shall see, it is a tremendously difficult feat to love someone for themselves, and separate from ourselves. Adults are able to do it only intermittently, and with much effort. For the child, particularly the infant, that he can even momentarily accept his mother's separateness and can, at the same time, retain his loving feelings for her (albeit with difficulty and an admixture of hostile feelings) is nothing short of miraculous.

Of course, the very mention of sexuality in connection with motherhood is taboo. We know where babies come from, but once they're here we like to forget it. Juxtaposition of the words "sexual love" and "mother and child" contains inherent shock value. Just as the notion that love and sexuality themselves derive from the world of the child's body, indistinguishably, disturbs a great many people.

28

It was not so very long ago that the model of "pure"—
that is, non-physical, non-sexual—love was supposed to be
the love between mother and child. Somehow it was considered that what passed between them was in the nature
of a spiritual transaction. This conveniently neglected the
fundamental reality that a major part of the care which the
baby demands and mother bestows involves functions that
are entirely physical and body-centered, that little in the
way of abstract thinking need come out of what happens
between them, that essentially it is one body taking care of,
stimulating, and, in turn, being stimulated by, another,
much smaller body. As for the "higher" values implicit in
all of this, ask any mother with three kids under five years
of age, at about four o'clock in the afternoon, just how
exalted is her loving role. If she happens to be dealing with
one of their more elemental functions at the time, may I
suggest that you ask your questions from a safe and respect-
ful distance.

In fact, it is precisely these details of maternal caring at
so earthly and elemental a level, so involved with feeding
or with getting rid of wastes, that flesh out the sexual loving that the relationship of mother and child really is. It is
a sexual relationship not only for the child whose body receives care and love but also for the mother whose body
gives it. We shall see later how this is experienced from the
mother's point of view.

For now, it's important to underline the basic identity
of love and sexuality for the child. Love and sex begin as
one. It is only later, in adulthood, that there is a distinction
between the two. And for adults, the problem, simply
stated, is the overcoming of that distinction and the re-
creation of the childhood world of sexual loving, but with a
difference—the added complexity of adult sexuality.

Popular simplifiers of sexuality do little to help solve the dilemma. In their writings they like to divide love and sex. I am thinking specifically of advice-giving columnists, such as Ann Landers, whose oversimplifications are a balm to that mass of people who can tolerate only simple answers. But they are worse than a disservice; they are a genuine injury to the many who earnestly seek enlightenment and whose desperation drives them to Miss Landers and her colleagues. Sex, they say, is a biologic drive, whereas love is an emotion. Personally, I'm not certain how this makes for any distinction between the two, but for these apologists it seems to mean that sex is some kind of crude, raw energy (like crude oil), whereas love is somehow on a higher plane, educated, cultivated. This kind of reasoning allows one to conclude that there need never be, nor ever have been, any genuine relationship between the two and that we learn to connect love and sex, presumably in conformity with our society's values, and through the blessings of matrimony. In reality, the reverse is true. Sex and love have common origins and would be inextricably related were it not for the process of learning and development in this culture which teaches us to split the two.

This intimate connection between love and sexuality and their relation, in origin and development, to the mother's responsiveness were beautifully demonstrated in the laboratory some years ago when Dr. Harry Harlow set out to define the nature of mother love.

His now famous experiments consisted of removing newborn monkeys from their natural mother and putting them in a cage with two different kinds of mechanical mother—that is, manmade objects that could provide food, warmth, and, in the case of one of these (a form wrapped in terry cloth), even bodily-contact comfort. His original intent was to isolate those factors essential to life sustenance in mothering. The whole question of the fabled mother-child relationship was up for re-examination. He found that he could indeed supplant the need for a real mother and that monkeys would accept a terry-cloth model as a substitute, and thrive. But a curious thing happened to these monkeys on their way to maturity. Socially, they could not get along at all in the world of other monkeys. And sexually they were total duds. The male monkeys brought up on terry-cloth mothers never reproduced. And only a very few females raised this way could be cajoled to permit sexual contact. And then only with the most suave and understanding normal monkeys. Finally, these females, when they were able to conceive at all, made really poor mothers, neglecting their infants, seemingly unaware of them as living beings, unable to care for them in the slightest degree. It was necessary to introduce foster-mother monkeys to keep the babies of mother-deprived monkeys alive. Harlow set out to question the importance of the living presence of the mother to the child. His work provides evidence that the mother, in her continued dealings with the child, not only provides something beyond physical care that makes life possible but also that specialized adult social and sexual functions, reproductive functions, and parenting functions do not develop adequately in her absence. At least for monkeys, it is clearly established that mother love and the relationship of the child to that love underlie the development of adult sexuality.

What does the real mother provide that the terry-cloth mother does not? It's not the milk, the warmth, the security of her presence. All these can be duplicated. What the real mother does provide is the conflict that grows out of her own inability to meet her baby's every need. In other words, sometimes she must frustrate and even punish her baby; she does not only say "yes" in her living interactions, she also says "no." I am tempted to add: because, after all, she's only human. By which we mean imperfect. And her imperfections set the stage for the growth and development that comes partly as a response to the limits she must set, and partly as a response to the good feelings and "basic trust" generated by her own attempts to meet her child's needs and wishes and demands in spite of everything. Mother's human failings—her inability to satisfy the child completely—bring him closer to the reality that he is not all-powerful. After all, here are his needs unmet. Here is discomfort, and try as he may, it won't be willed away. The state of displeasure brings him closer to the reality that there is another being in the world, separate from himself—mother—and that she is responsible for bringing him pleasure, for keeping pain away. As long as she is successful in satisfying him, there's no point in recognizing her separate existence. That recognition comes about, at least partially, as a result of pain and discontent. It is an unpleasant recognition. The child experiences that sense of disturbance, of inner disbalance, which we call anxiety. To experience that feeling of separateness is to feel helpless and vulnerable. In the child's world, it opens him up to the threat of annihilation. And so, recognizing his separateness from mother when she fails him, he does everything he can to wipe it out, to deny that truth.

Here is where you can see what I meant when I said that the struggle between the child's wished-for omnipotence and his actual helplessness acts as a spur to his learning and his growth. To try to overcome the truth of his separateness he really must begin "to use his head." He develops the use of fantasy, the construction of meaningful images and formed and directed inner experience.

Fantasy develops as a response to the separation from the loved one, from mother. In her absence—or, what amounts to the same thing, her failure to satisfy his needs—the child first "hallucinates" her. His strong belief in the good feelings she evokes first leads him to the view that it is his own doing, that her coming to his rescue is a coming at his bidding, just like the laboratory mice who "trained" their keeper. With time, mother must fail to keep her promises, and when she does not show up in the flesh to meet the child's demands, he reinvents her in spirit, in an image of her that he has built in his mind. In the absence of physical satisfaction from mother herself, the image of her in fantasy can sustain and support him in relative satisfaction for a limited time. This act, the transition from the "real" mother as a means of gratification to the use of the image of her in fantasy, is prototypical for the later development of more elaborate fantasy and complex imagery. The development of imagination, creativity, the capacity to play, indeed, the development of intellection in all forms of abstraction, are outgrowths of this primary experience.

To learn, the child must experience the sense of well-being that comes from adequate care; he must also experience the frustration that comes from care that fails at some point to meet every need. If he is not cared for, he will not have the emotional strength to strive; if he is never frustrated, he need not give a damn.

A mother complained to several doctors of her five-year-old's failure to speak. Examinations yielded the fact that he was a remarkably healthy child, and she was told not to worry. But worry she did. One day, in a hurry, she burned his oatmeal but served it anyway. He tasted it, spat it out, and said, "God, this stuff is awful. You must have burned it." Delighted, she said, "You're talking! Why haven't you said anything before this?" He looked at her with some disdain and said, "Well, everything's been all right up to now!"

The growth of fantasy and, later, of cognitive functioning begins as a response to separation or the threat of separation. Since anxiety is what we feel, what we experience inside our bodies, at the threat of separation, it is correct to say that fantasy begins as a means of ameliorating anxiety, as a kind of mental pacifier which the child constructs to soothe himself, to keep anxiety at a minimum. It is an attempt to bring back the momentarily lost feelings of loving union with mother. In that sense, fantasy and learning are an early substitute for love (granted, fantasy and learning may also function later to acquire love, to retain love, or simply for the pleasure and love of themselves).

That fledgling ability to fantasy is dependent upon the child's "faulty" grasp of the ways things "really" are, his view of the loving world as being an integral part of himself. The building of fantasy happens easily within that world as a way of bringing back any part of the world that may elude his grasp and will, or of compensating him for its loss. So fantasy quiets the feeling of distress, the anxiety of separation and the loss of love, by building an internal world of love, denying the truth, that he is alone. And so, all's right again. For a time.

But while fantasy soothes the child, and helps him deal

with separation, it also separates him, in another sense, from the mother, and her closeness in loving union.

Fantasy and the intellection which later elaborates from it, serves the paradoxical function of keeping reality from us and, at the same time, of bringing it to us. It helps to deny anxiety and the reality of separation, thus fostering the building of an inner, unreal world in which we continue to dream our dream of domination and have our wishes served. But by developing better tools, abstraction and intellection, with which to "grasp" the external world, fantasy eventually serves the purpose of anchoring us in external reality and finally forcing us to confront our individuality and separateness.

For the child, in helping to build an inner world of satisfactions, fantasy helps him endure mother's absence for longer and longer periods, periods during which he is engaged instead with her image and then with other independent thoughts. So that fantasy helps to shape the basis of his increasingly real separateness and individuality. In a future time he will have available his own inner world of fantasy as a place to withdraw from other relationships, people who come upon the loving scene after mother, when they, too, fail to satisfy.

In addition to the use of fantasy, learning comes about in yet another way in connection with the threat of separation and loss. Because of his prolonged dependence, and the indulgent dreams stimulated by mother's loving care, the child, as we saw, was peculiarly vulnerable to the self-deceit of *his* omnipotent control of her. Any threat to that unreal sense of reality was experienced as anxiety; fantasy and the rudiments of organized intellect developed as a means of survival to keep anxiety at a minimum. This same vulnerability makes it possible for the mother to make demands upon the child, demands that he behave in conformity with her wishes or face the threat of the loss of her.

Dr. Urie Bronfenbrenner, the developmental psychologist, has remarked what a formidable tool for socialization is the threat of the loss of love, what enormous power the parent or other caretaker has over the child to bend its wishes and impulses to that parental will, whether the socializing force is the parent of the individual family as in the United States or the collective will of the group and of society as in the U.S.S.R. The greater the gratification that has been given, the more effective is the threat of its loss in bringing the child in line.

And so he proceeds. To do her bidding. To delay his gratification of one impulse or another so as not to lose the best of them all, for of course, as he grows and develops, as his ego system and his nervous system and muscular system develop, he becomes aware that that which he loves, that which satisfies his needs, that which provides his sense of good inner feelings, his mother, is actually separate and outside of him. And in trying to keep those good feelings, he grows by learning. Each step taking him further and further away from her, as if in a paradox of loving.

In one important sense, living experience, from birth to death, is a history of increasing competence and mastery, as well as simultaneous successive losses, each step in growth accompanied by a corresponding loss in the dependent tie. Birth is the moment of independent life, but it is also the loss of the global satisfactions that were present before. The milestones of development which dot childhood are also markers of loss. Mother helps the child to learn to drink from a bottle or a cup, and he must give up the breast in his weaning. The child learns to walk. And is delighted. And so are the parents who helped him to pick himself up. But soon he is carried less. Even the firm support of the floor must be given up when we assume the erect position, and we must rely upon our relatively weak spines for what was formerly offered to our four-leggedness with ease. Talking is achieved, and never again can we expect to be interpreted, to be totally understood, without making an effort to express ourselves exactly. All this happens very slowly, of course—else how could it be borne? But it happens. Each growing step, in response to the wish for love, in the gift of love, in the loss of the frail dependence that makes the total loving union of mother necessary in the first place. Each step in growth is accompanied by the joy and happiness of accomplishment, and by the pain and sadness of loss. That is something which is difficult to grasp. But we do not accept the separation that comes with growth without struggle. And just as we cry at birth for largely physiologic reasons, our tears which later we learn to see as part of frustration and rage come quickly as we are thrust into each new phase of development.

Individuation goes on throughout a lifetime. The body as structural space may be an entity at birth, separate from others; the body as emotional space will never, without great hazard, achieve total independence. But a process of becoming a self, an individual, will go on.

An early part of growing into one's selfhood is marked by knowing one's name. It is still another step to be able to articulate that name. And the stages along the way are visible if we care to look. My two-year-old son responds when I call "Sammy"; he comes to me or stops pulling on the cat's tail, depending on my inflection. But this ability is a primitive sign of his developing uniqueness. He also shares this capacity for responding to signals with humbler animals and their less complex nervous systems. My dog can come as quickly or even quicker. He is fully grown and this response is the best he can do; he does it well. After a time, Sammy learns to say "Daddy." And I'm suitably impressed. A little later he adds "Mommy." To her disappointment at being second named. After all, who cares for him all of the time? Who sees to it his needs are met almost as soon as they are expressed? Mommy is puzzled that he takes longer to give her symbolic recognition. His own name remains unarticulated. In spite of repeated attempts to elicit a mimicked "Sammy," the question "What's your name?" brings only silence. What can it mean?

It centers on the issue of space. My child can articulate a word that stands powerfully for *me* quite early. He sees me as a large person who comes and goes each day in his life. Daddy goes to work and we say "bye bye!" Daddy comes home and there's a little excitement. In Sammy's world Daddy is constantly on the go. And separate. And unavailable during part of the day when he'd like to play. Mommy, on the other hand, is old reliable herself. For a long time, she's there practically every waking minute. Mostly, if there's any leaving, it's Sammy who does it, when he goes to sleep. Sammy controls things. He cries in the morning, announcing his wakefulness, and she appears. Or has a tantrum with his food, and she does something to make it better. Daddy can't be summoned up that way. It takes but little to see that Daddy is separate. But Mommy is something else. How does it become apparent that she is an individual, apart from Sammy? Mostly through frustration. The times she does not respond as quickly as he'd like.

Moments when she is not gratifying, but meets his wish with another of her own perhaps, forcing him to yield. The times she is divided from him by her attention to other people, other demands, Daddy, the outside world. So slowly, and in anger, it dawns upon him that she is different, separate, and, uncertainly, he gives her a name, "Mommy." To name Sam as "Sam" would require a detachment from himself that is much slower to develop. To say "Sam" would imply that he is somewhere outside of "Sam." He can say "Daddy" and has become certain of the notion that Daddy is separate from Sam because Daddy comes and goes. So, too, Mommy comes and goes, albeit less obviously, but with even greater emotional impact. He can say "Mommy," for Mommy is also separate from Sam. But if he says "Sam," perhaps Sam will come and go and be separate from Sam. Perhaps, indeed, Sam will disappear. It is anxiety which prohibits this naming of himself. It is the anxiety of all risk taking. Of the first step in anything. In this case it is the anxiety of becoming an abstraction, the self.

Lest we lose sight of the real world, and fall prey to the child's own solipsistic version and see the world only through his eyes, we must credit the mother with her unique view of the child's growing abilities and his waning childhood. And try to feel *her* feelings.

The early feelings of tenderness, of closeness, of sensual holding, cuddling, cohesion with warmth, providing warmth, receiving warmth, give way to the drained anguish of depletion and the gnawing doubts of not giving enough, not having enough to give, not wanting to give all and everything. And the joy of caring for infantile helplessness mingles with the overwhelming reality of its burdensome-

ness. And the timelessness. The structureless vagueness—
hypnotic. The sense of falling herself into an abyss of infantile longing. The sense of disorganization. All quickly
torn into mobilized purpose when the child cries, demanding care, and she must run quickly and efficiently through
her diagnostic checklist and come up with the right and
satisfying answer. And she does. So often. So often. But she
must tire. She must become bored. She is faced with other
demands in the world. And her other needs. And so she
fails. And feels the pain of failing. And his anger at her
failure. And her own anger at being so often challenged.

Her anger helps to keep her anchored firmly in her own
reality, a reality which must touch on the world beyond her
child. Her caretaking love of her child makes the dual demand on her inner resources of complementing the child's
neediness with her ministrations and, at the same time,
identifying with him and his needs in order to know what
to do in the first place. Both of these demands, for comple-
mentarity and identity with her child draw her seductively
into his universe, to fall partial prey to his powerful view of
her as only a part, a helpful part, but *only* a part, of his
world. It is a genuine temptation to share and support this
unreal view of things, but the countless and unceasing demands finally provoke her to satisfy her needs and to refuse,
in anger, his every demand, yielding to those she can more
reasonably fulfill, and finally turning things around to make
her demands the more powerfully willed ones.

She must experience and express this anger in order both
to survive and to make possible her child's growth. We
don't hear much about anger as an *aid* to child rearing.
More of the emphasis has been given to *understanding* the
child, speaking *his* language, satisfying *his* needs. And of

course gratifying him *is* important and necessary. But it can be only half the picture, if that picture is to be anything like the way things can really be for humans. Human mothers, like monkey mothers, or other mothers, can never be all "give"; and when, from loving motives and finally from angry ones, they demand of their child, in turn, behavior that furthers his independence, the forestalling of the immediacy of his insistence, the delay of his gratification, they manage at the same time to speed him along his path and to teach him better how to cope.

At a minimum, coping is taught simply through the child's experience of his mother's anger. He learns then that anger is permissible, that there are means of expressing and experiencing anger in oneself and others. After all, if *she* can be angry and the whole world doesn't crumble, then maybe he can be safe in it a little while longer.

The world becomes finally a much more fearful place for the child whose mother is *never* angry in it.

The child experiences his mother's anger and his own as well. After all, he is faced with intolerable choices sometime early in his life. He can't bear the threat of losing mother, which is what her anger signifies to him. That means experiencing anxiety and a feeling of his own imminent destruction. To pacify himself and to keep anxiety at bay, he conjures up an image of her in fantasy, an image that is satisfying even when she is not. But that is only partially successful. Oh, yes, a thought of someone you love can be consoling, but it won't entirely keep away the gnawing of hunger, or the clamminess of being wet, or any number of discomforts and dissatisfactions, great and small, that punctuate everyday life. So when fantasy falls short, and the anxiety builds again, he converts his feeling of helplessness to one of rage. Instead of feeling hurt and vulnerable and needy and, most of all, deserted in his neediness, cast off, rejected by an angry mother, he turns the passivity into activity. He is the one who does the rejecting, in half-formed thoughts of "I'll show her." "I don't even want her." "I don't need her or anyone!"

His anger is a shield to the pain of loss. But implicitly it recognizes the loss, accepts it partially, establishing a distance between himself and her. For in his world "good" is a feeling that is inside himself, that *is* himself, while "bad" is extruded to the outside world. But, being angry with mother (and she with him), he banishes her to that world outside. And so accepts her individuality, and the love he extends to her, as separate from him. For the moment. In the next moment, yearning for her, he brings her back, in fantasy, grieving the loss of her. And the struggle continues, seesawing back and forth between his anger and his love as he erects boundaries between himself and her, creating in the fire of that anger the very margins of his inner self, extending their momentary differences into permanence, restructuring the way he looks at and works with the world.

Thus, anger and anxiety at the threatened loss of the sexual loving union with mother have a hand in the design of the boundaries of the child's emotional space. Each incident gives shape and texture and meaning to those inner defensive walls and, through the incomplete working of fantasy, lend color to what will be carried as memory, as pain and disappointment.

But mostly mother *is* gratifying. And mostly he is not angry but vulnerable to her and to the possibility of losing her. And so she is able to teach him to do more and more for himself. And he does. For her. For love of her. And grows away from her. Infancy's time dies. And mother can feel the pain and sadness at its passing, seeing the lost joys of their closeness, their sharing, and she holds on to the symbols of those days, the bracelet from the hospital nursery, the first baby shoes, the hair from his first barbering, carrying them with her to her own memory and her own pacifying fantasy.

Mother's love for her child is complex, convoluted. It is sexual in much the same way that the child's love of her is sexual. It is often confounded by the ease with which at every step in his growth she can get caught up in patterns of behavior which reflect issues still unsettled in her mature life. And the shape and expression of her love, and of what pains her in his growing steps, is altered to express those hidden strains in herself. But whatever the shape, whatever the form her feelings take, one reality must be confronted above all. Mothering is a losing game. And at its best mother's love must be the love of someone prepared to give up, prepared to help another to be free of her.

Of course, mother is not alone simply giving, giving, in her relationship with the child, although, to hear the many authorities on child development, she might as well be. We have emphasized her role and function because it is so largely within *its* context that the child's sexuality is cast, and his vulnerability to anxiety, and his capacity for hatred. There is mother's side of it, and we have only lightly touched upon it here, the way in which she is gratified in sexual loving from what goes on between her and her child.

The relationship of the child to the pleasures of *his* body is the sexuality of childhood; and love is the relationship of the child to that which gives him pleasure, his body. It is also the extension of feeling to the person whose intimate caring for the child and his body makes life and pleasure happen, his mother. The mother's experience of the child is also a part of her sexuality. Because her sexual world is grown-up, and therefore narrowed in the scope of its expression to genital experiences, we tend toward revulsion at the idea of a sexual liaison between her and her child. But just as the pleasure she gives him forms the root structure of his world and his sexuality, so pleasure she derives is a substantial sexual experience—but it is only a part of her sexual expression. In her adulthood she has come to accept certain sensual experiences as sexual when they are in a context which she can allow herself to associate with fulfillment through intercourse or in other ways appropriate to time and place. Although the sexuality of the universe is there, as it is for anyone, for the taking, she rarely reaches for it, busying herself with the world of her work. Unlike the child, she seldom wiggles her toes, stares with her eyes, or listens to her intestinal rumblings for the sheer pleasure of it. So many bodily experiences are suppressed, taken for granted, ignored, and never come into serious contention for possible sexual gratification.

But some experiences she cannot ignore. And they arise between her and her child. The act of birth, if she is conscious, is a vastly sexual experience, and many women honest with themselves and with their bodies have admitted orgasmic experiences as a result of the passage of the newborn through "the portals of life." After all, if it is possible for a woman to be gratified through the repeated thrusting of a penis in and out of her vagina, but coming into her from the outside, it makes perfect sense that the same mounting rhythmic pressure applied from within should do no less.

The sucking of her breast can easily be a part of a woman's adult lovemaking; when the smiling face of her baby is responsible, the mouth nibbling hungrily for its life's food, it is still a sexual experience. And if mother won't admit it, her body will betray her. We know that the suckling of her child quickens the return of her flaccid uterus to its former firmness. The message gets around the body from the pleasured breast, starting contractions in the pelvis, in the womb. The body is limited in the number and kinds of responses it can make. One set of contractions, say, in response to a child at the breast is as good as another, say, in response to one's lover. But the mind has unlimited means for rationalizing, for denial, for helping us to fool ourselves that, after all, it's not sexual. Sexual is intercourse is fucking is animal is dogs in the street is dirty is forbidden. Isn't it? Between mother and child? For shame!

And what to say to the impulse she has, bending over her naked child, to kiss, to lick, his genitals? What? It never happens! That's terrible! Why, that's like grown-up people. It's disgusting!

But sexuality is potentially a two-way street. And if it's mama's pleasuring of him that lets the child love his body, his world, how could we believe she has no stake, no pleasure in it? Or that the pleasure is somehow "mother love," as if by saying that we meant something devoid of humanity, sterile of life.

If the child's experience of mother is sexual in the diffuse sense we have described, her pleasure is the more obviously sexual, in the terms by which we conventionally define it, in terms of the genital responsiveness of adults. But her pleasure is also, like the child's, the diffuse delight in the

45

activities of the body, stimulated to a greater extent than before she became a mother by the bodily events which follow on conception. To a significant extent, her dealings with her child and, before his actual birth, with her body, which contains his, re-create the earliest of her own physical memories and renew her capacity for joy in the stimulation of her body's processes. She is drawn into that sexual world of childhood and its enormous sensitivity to stimuli. And a conflict is engendered between the diffuse pleasure that that childhood world contains for her in her body and the more focal one which is hers as an adult, the pleasure of the genitals. That conflict, as we shall see, is often played out in her relationship with her lover, with the father of the child, and often with disastrous results.

For the loving sexual union of mother and babe does indeed have a tendency toward exclusiveness, a tendency which she must resist. As we saw, mother, seen as part of the child's universe, becomes *mother* to the child as an outgrowth of his love for himself and of his actual helplessness and limited ability to apprehend reality. The fact of her separateness was met by adaptive maneuvers produced by his unwillingness to look at and accept her separateness. For mother, the same problem is felt on a different level. She knows she is not just *a part* of his world. She perceives that she may be nearly *all* of his world. She must somehow make it clear to herself and to the rest of her family that *he* is not *all* of *her* world.

Fortunately she has the rest of the real world to help her and the strongest demand of the real world, the father. Father, if only by expressing his needs and making his demands upon her, provides a stability, an anchor in the real world. Usually he does much more. He gives his loving support to her and to the child, and he builds his own bridges to his baby. He brings in elements from the working life outside the home that help to mark the passage of time and to put events in perspective in the family's life. But if he were to do little else but demand his due, if he were to be nothing more than selfish, it would serve the laudable purpose of forcing some separation of child and mother and so of promoting growth. And growth carries with it the opportunity of newness and its risk of the loss of the old. And thus implicitly its risk of loss of ourselves. For the old *is* what we know of ourselves.

And so, anxiety.

2

Love and Sex for Adults

I'VE TRIED to give a plausible and useful ordering to the growth of love and human sexuality from its origins in childhood. The central concept was the idea of change and growth as simultaneous loss and acquisition, bitter and sweet, but in any case I have stressed the importance of moving the child along toward the separateness of the adult, able to love because he has been loved, and able to hate and to be sad because he has lost that love as well, and still survived, living with anxiety.

All this time I have been talking about the way things work in "normal" people, people whose lives are otherwise uneventful but for the trauma of birth within a (Western) human family.

Love and sexuality ought to proceed simply and easily. Become more complex and convoluted as adolescence succeeds childhood and then be more elaborated in adulthood. But somehow it's not so easy to define. Those who have tried to describe and define adult love and adult sexuality have repeatedly failed. From Socrates, who saw love as a kind of mad frenzy, to modernists, who have tried to deny its meaningful existence or have romanticized it with hot buttered schmaltz.

Maybe it's easier to talk about kids because they are smaller and their worlds are smaller. In many ways their problems are more nearly identical—if only because their range of available choices is limited. As we grow, we do attain a measure of uniqueness and so it becomes harder to generalize about sex and love in adulthood because each adult has his own version.

Yet it is worth trying to unravel the problem in the hope not of providing definitive answers but of asking useful and guiding questions.

I began by describing the difficulty of encounter, the anxious first moments of engagement between lovers. Let's begin again there but grant that they have met and have fallen in love. Just how love happens we'll ignore for now. Assume it does. We are, after all, really interested in what happens afterward, when the curtain has fallen on the lovers' bliss.

At the outset everything is ecstasy. Love has a way of painting the sky the right shade of blue, of making people want to rhyme "June" and "moon." Suddenly your senses are expanding. You hear music in a way you never did. Individual notes with clarity and precision. Time seems to be suspended. Even the laws of gravity, if not repealed, are debatable. Well, they seem negotiable. You see, hear, feel, touch, smell, a whole new and greater world. Your body is alive and beautiful.

Sound like a drug trip? It is a trip. Into inner and outer space at the same time. Because suddenly, perhaps without being able to articulate it, you are aware of the reason for your existence. You are to *be*. And together with your love it's all right to *be*.

Most lovers are too busy loving to say much about it, but a creative few were somehow able to perceive themselves and later tell the rest of us. One thing that takes place is an ordering of your consciousness, an expansion of it to include another, as well as a lack of focus on yourself; you have lost your self-consciousness. You have gained, instead, a sense of *being* greater somehow than the individual you are. You have become slightly exalted.

O.K. Loving is beautiful. And it goes along like that for a time. And then, things begin to change. Suddenly, little things begin to make a difference. Your perfect love becomes flawed before your eyes, like a metal plate corroded in an acid bath. Small irritations become major grievances. Little differences grow to big conflicts. And instead of peaceful loving you feel an evil and a wish to stop it all and to get away. You fight and maybe you do get away. If you do come back, the old perfection may be gone. Maybe permanently. In its place may be resignation. Or a new level of acceptance. Or nothing.

And sexually, change is the word that describes your life. You begin with an excitement that is so much a part of your loving. But in a while it seems to die, to be gone. And you don't know why. And you wonder if it's you. Or if it's him. Or if it's her. And if it does come back—your excitement—it's surprising intensity makes everything seem right again, brings back the loving and the joy. Even the blue sky and the sense of being whole and together. Until it goes again. Or you hate again. And you wonder if you're going crazy. Or why no one told you love would be like this.

To begin with encounter, with the meeting of strangers trying to become intimates. It's true that two people meeting for the first time, in the hope of something more, of love and of sex between them in some future time, a moment away, are afraid. Like Lucille, whom we met, crying about it because she can't overcome her fears. Like ourselves. They're afraid because of long-standing personal memories of fear and even more ancient racial ones. The fear of loving. Love implies vulnerability to the loss of love. And anxiety at the threat must be warded off, with anger, or with the mental work of fantasy, or with a hundred little defensive maneuvers that are part of each person's own stock in trade. Part of their safety equipment, operating at their personal boundaries.

Loving for children happens quite naturally. It comes with the territory, you might say, of their own bodies. And so does infantile sexuality, as we defined it. The child loves himself and he loves his mother because to him they are one and the same. Gradually it dawns upon him that she is really outside and he continues to love as he has extended his feelings to her. Even outside of him she still represents him, still exerts an effect upon his inner sense of well-being with her slightest look, her mildest indisposition. He feels her feelings as his own. The important task of growing up is the ability to learn to love, first mother, then others, as separate beings.

Loving for adults re-creates the earliest experiences of childhood with all the possibilities for happiness and pain. The good feelings come from the sense of being at one with another. The painful ones from the awareness of vulnerability to loss.

Love is a threat to one's boundaries.

Small wonder, then, that the moment of encounter contains so much anxiety. Because what the boundaries guard and contain are the limits of each person's inner territory, his emotional space, his sense of his uniqueness. It is this sense of himself which he has won at such great cost in the process of becoming adult. And the cost of gaining it has been the successive losses of loved ones in some degree, and of deeply held hopes. Every instance of separation and acceptance of his mortal fragility has led him closer to the realization of himself, starting with mother and the acknowledgment of *her* separate existence. Every loss and the threat of loss was accompanied by anxiety at the experience of his helplessness. And in warding off the anxiety he worked at producing the very self he now has and is, and the very boundaries that contain it. With each successive loss in development he experienced anger and sadness and the fantasies and wishes that life were not so, and he attempted through new and learned behavior to *make* it not so; and by creating boundaries of defense and of outlook, to protect against the pain of loss and guard against future losses, he has altered his way of looking at the world, narrowed his range of choices, and focused his attempts at mastery of it, and of himself, and of meaningful engagement with the world of others.

And a new person, especially one who engages, who is interesting, threatens that delicate adjustment, threatens to come in through those boundaries, those barriers of defense. Into your inner field, where God knows what havoc may arise. Especially when your inner self is somehow hidden to you too. Or, worse yet, when what you do know about yourself is frightening.

The relaxation of boundaries can come about only when

you know you're not going to lose everything. You are not going to lose whatever is important to you—yourself, or your will, or your secrets. And when you are secure in the knowledge that if you do let someone in, to inspect your private dwelling place, what he will see is something you can like and respect.

Ordinarily the relaxing of personal boundaries takes time. Gradually you learn to trust this other person and to let him in to much that is private and personal to you. And he shares with you the territory of his own emotional space. That sharing in mutuality we call friendship. With more time and more intimacy it may even give over to love, and the sharing of selves becomes indistinguishable from loving in almost all respects.

But let's look for a moment at another kind of experience, one that does not always happen gradually. In fact, its suddenness and intensity have given poets substance for their art and scientists something to trouble over. Instead of barriers being gradually reduced, they seem swept away in a rush of feeling. And we call *that* feeling "love," and describe what happens as "falling in love." And the lovers call that moment when the barriers, so quickly swept away, return again—"betrayal."

Why people fall in love will continue to mystify for quite some time. Surely it is a matter of highly individualized experience and the accidents of the moment. People give such a wide range of reasons, if that is any help at all, for their falling in love. From the physical to the abstract. Smell. Appearance. Hair length. Eye color. Vocal tones. Vocabulary. Thoughtfulness. Gentleness. Moreover, the time that the two lovers meet has to be just right. You may meet the same person at one time in your life and hardly notice, then chance upon him or her later and fall head over heels. The difference is in the readiness of lovers to love.

It's impossible to generalize successfully about the characteristics that are the *bases* for producing the feelings and emotional shiftings of falling in love. Beauty is in the eyes of the beholder. And what is seen as beautiful and lovable depends upon that beholding eye and the individual experience logged by the brain behind it. Dr. John Money of Johns Hopkins has theorized that falling in love for humans may be a variation of the process of "imprinting," a phenomenon observed in many mammals and made famous by the naturalist Konrad Lorenz. Lorenz proved that he could get baby ducklings to follow him, single-file, the way they normally would a mother duck, if he but waddled past them during a few critical hours of their immediate postnatal life. Dr. Money feels that falling in love may depend upon a similar process in humans, in which the stimulating attributes of an important influencing person will become incorporated in some crucial life moment and later serve as a signal to love when they are rediscovered in a suitable potential lover. Then, Zap!

While imprinting as a process has not been conclusively demonstrated as the *basis* for any human behavior, the selection of particular characteristics that are found later in a lover may often take place early in life. One of my patients reported that long after he had met and married "the woman of his dreams," he found an old photograph of his mother as a very young girl. The resemblance was remarkable.

On the basis of what I have said about the growth of love and sexuality within the context of the relationship of the child and his mother, it might be possible to conclude that all love affairs ought to be like that one. That we consistently select as a lover someone who reminds us of that early loving. And I would agree, saving only that what is remembered and what is later recognized anew in the lover need not be any particular set of physical characteristics. Something happens between them to make it possible for the barriers to dissolve. And when *that* happens, the original experience *is* re-created.

The readiness to fall in love is not so sharply individual a matter as are the qualities sought after. People are more likely to fall in love during periods of some kind of upheaval, some kind of change in their lives, mostly in the early stages of that change. It may be a change that is physical in origin or in effect. It may be an alteration of status. Or it may be a change in one's relationship to others in the world. Thus adolescence is a great time for loving. Or when college begins, or when it ends. Or when you've just been promoted to vice-president. Or simply when you go away on vacation.

All of these shifts offer a challenge and create a tension, requiring new consciousness of yourself, and a new alignment of the energies used to maintain your personal boundaries. And under the stress of the change you become a little more vulnerable, a little more available. You experience a heightened sense of yourself as an individual and at the same time a greater willingness to let go of that isolation. It's almost as though, having accepted the conflict of a new situation, one that seems to occur naturally, that is almost of your choosing, the battle has already shifted. The very fact of confrontation with a changed reality implies that something—reality itself—has passed beyond your boundaries and into your inner world, at least to a degree. And being busy dealing with the change inside leaves you peculiarly vulnerable to the acceptance of a new challenge at the boundaries.

But when a new challenge is presented, in the form of a potential lover, the anxiety is still there, at the edge of encounter. It is only less effective, as *you* are less effective, being preoccupied with the taxing inner work of adaptation. Anxiety remains because the process of falling in love is well named. It is a "fall," from a present state to an experience of a state that has gone before. It is, like dreaming, like becoming crazy, like getting high on LSD, a process of regression. That is its beauty as well as its perceived danger to us. And because of what a regressive shift means to us, we guard against it with anxiety.

A regression is a step backward through our own emotional time, a kind of science-fiction device which we all possess, to move, as through a time warp, back to an earlier stage in emotional experience. Here you are. One moment you're an adult. In the next you're suddenly a kid again. One moment you have all that control, that sensibility, that relative certainty of decision making, born of your individual (and painfully gained) experience. Next you're flooded with uncertainty, confusion, and that strange acute awareness and sensitivity of childhood.

Remember how, when you were a kid, the world of adults was a strangely transparent place. Adults spoke words at one another, made noise, said things. But sometimes they seemed to be feeling things quite different from what they said with their words. Sometimes contradictory things, those words and those feelings. And you, the child, could hear the words and somehow hear the feelings too. Although the adults could hear only one at a time. You felt like someone who has access to a secret code. It made adults at one and the same time simple to understand and confusing. Why did they hide or, rather, pretend to hide their feelings from one another? Why did they agree among themselves not to look, not to recognize each other's emotions? And why did they get so mad if you, naïvely, interfered and "spoke out of turn," telling the truth as you felt it about them?

If you can remember experiences like these from your childhood, then chances are you're still in contact with a bit of the ego feeling of childhood, the acute consciousness of attitudes and feelings in others, that has led to one clinician's pithy saying: "The child doesn't just hear the words; he hears the music too."

This sensitivity which children possess is gradually buried as we grow to adulthood. Their openness is more than empathy. Empathy is a grown-up way of experiencing what others do, a deliberate putting of oneself in another's shoes. The empathy of grownups is achieved through intentional disciplined effort; the ability of kids to feel what others do comes easy, almost effortlessly. Sometimes, because what they experience in this way is so uncomfortable, it may almost be against their will that they take on the feeling.

Originally, in childhood, the ego feelings are much greater than they are destined to become with maturity. The ego of the child does not have the defined boundaries of later life. The oceanic feeling of personal limitlessness which is experienced represents a quality of being open, of being not closed, of being closer, more joined with other human beings. Such an ego is obviously more vulnerable, more unstable, more susceptible to influence, more shakable through the disruptions and upheavals of emotions. The openness and fluidity allow many more impressions to come into inner awareness, make possible a potential richness of imagery and impression. But what is taken in is not highly organized. Such an ego can absorb with great gusto, or reject flatly, but it cannot easily deal in gradations. Loving is easy. Hating is easy. But the gray areas between are difficult. The child feels intensely. And expresses it. But he forms dispassionate judgments only with difficulty. That is the function of developing ego boundaries as he grows. To create a finer system of discrimination about the inner and outer world. And so, with maturity he loses that boundless sensitivity and gains, instead, a steadier sense of himself. But not forever and always.

When an adult enters a new situation, or is suddenly confronted with a group of strangers, he may feel a sudden confusion, perhaps even terror. He may instantaneously and momentarily lose contact with himself. He may feel people will reject him, because for the moment he feels worthless and rejectable. And his actions will betray his uncertainty. And we may say of him that he is insecure. He is. He is uncertain of *himself*. Under the stress of the novelty or the pressure of meeting many new strangers, he experiences an almost totally involuntary opening of his ego boundaries, a sense that others are forcing themselves in upon him, or a feeling of impending annihilation. Perhaps, unsure of how to set limits upon those around him, unsure of how to shore up his personal boundaries, he may feel as if "he is falling apart."

Adult "stranger anxiety" is only one of the many common regressive experiences we all endure. There are many

others, some quite ordinary, some not. To fall asleep and
to dream is one of the more commonplace regressions. The
laws of logic, of causality, of relationship, as we know them
in waking life, become suspended. Anything can happen in
our dreams for any reason.

Adults routinely experience a regression when they travel
for an extended time in a foreign country and attempt to
fit into its customs and to learn a new language. Suddenly
they are two years old again, placing nouns where predi-
cates ought to be, committing gaffes and blunders willy-
nilly. Saying things like "Don't take apart me the luggage!"
when they mean "Please put all my bags together." The
whole complex of responses for which we have invented a
special phrase, "culture shock." A disruption, incidentally,
which is less troublesome for children with their still yielding boundary systems.

Sometimes people may actively seek such an experience
by taking a drug like LSD or undergoing the discipline of
one of the ways of meditation. For them, the laws of time
and space are temporarily abrogated and a minute feels like
an hour, or two things *can be* in the same place at the same
time. And most importantly, the temporal and spatial limits
of the self are for the time being erased.

And then there is the unwanted accident of developing
insanity. That is the most stark example of regression, one
that is not so easy to reverse. Throughout the ages, poets
and philosophers have intuitively linked insanity and love.
Even today, what psychiatrists understand as insanity, psy-
chosis, is a serious failure to grasp and interact with the
reality of the world. What "falling in love" has in common
with becoming insane and with the other more acceptable
forms of regression, of dreaming, of transplantation to a

different land, of discovery of a new "high," is the sudden loss of control over the personal boundaries, over the ego barrier that guards an individual's inner space, the very means he employs for screening and interpreting the outside world and for modulating his interactions with that world.

When you begin to relax the boundaries of your intimate space, you give up some of the control over your own coping mechanisms and with that loss of control comes a renewal of that old experience of helplessness which you endured as a child and which you experienced anew at every threat of separation and loss along the way to adulthood. This time the loss that is threatened is *you*. Or, more exactly, the adult you, the "uptight" you, or the "cool" you, or whatever you are as a mature and competent self, satisfied in your hard-won independence, reasonably content with the person you are and the gains and accomplishments in living ability that you wrested from the struggle for adulthood.

Sometimes that return of anxiety is enough to convince you that you are not so well-equipped to continue the struggle, that you really are helpless. That you need the help of another. And rather than face any longer the anxiety of being alone, you would prefer to give up that independence and cling instead to that other. And that may be enough to satisfy you, for the moment. To cling dependently, and call it love, when it is actually a running from yourself.

I said earlier that love is not founded in insufficiency, but in surfeit, in the love of oneself. The exception that proves the rule occurs at just those moments when, because of time or circumstance, the loving of oneself is already in question. Then one may make a premature decision, a

commitment to another, to love, to marry, say, a commitment founded on that momentary insecurity. And so the
love and the commitment depend for existence on that
sense of insufficiency. And may go when it goes.

A good example is the situation of the emerging adult,
the adolescent who commits himself to love or marriage
before he can be expected to be able to deal honestly. Commitment requires honesty. After all, honesty is nothing
more or less than *being clear*, clear about what you want,
clear about what you need, and clear about what you are
prepared to do and give in return—and then doing it. A
young person, in the middle of a struggle to gain his own
sense of identity, whose very integrity as an adult remains
incomplete, whose anxiety springs, to begin with, from the
basic question of who he is, is hardly in a position to be
honest in this sense. But in the midst of such a crisis of
identity, with so much at stake, so much uncertain and in
question, love may appear as an answer. And marriage may
follow right along.

The process of solidifying the sense of the self in adolescence is yet another of these normal crises of development
in which there is a heightening of the issues that generate,
and are in turn generated by, the individual's personal
boundaries. But at this particular time, with school and
work and autonomy and the body's demands all clamoring
for attention, there is a hurly-burly, a multiplicity of problems and possibilities. What will you do with your life?
What will you do to earn your place? What will be your
politics, your ideology, your esthetics, your religious pursuit?
What are you going to do with your sexual choices? And
what about the others, the people out there, the ones who
used to matter overmuch and now don't seem to, and the

ones who seem to matter even more? Questions upon questions, but they may be subsumed under three simple headings: Who am I? What have I been? What will I be?

And the feeling of anxiety emerges from them as he becomes aware, more aware than ever before, of the world about him and inside him, aware with an intensity that can leave him exhausted or running to the sanctuary of mental illness. Suddenly he is aware that it is *his* life. And *he* has to be responsible for it. And make decisions about it. Live it. And die in it. And that's a great deal of pain to feel, when you're young and you'd prefer to be invulnerable. To suddenly feel so mortal and so limited. It makes the growing person peculiarly inclined to look for easier solutions, more rapid resolutions of his own self-doubting, his own inability to reach decisions. Decisions are what adults make. And everyone knows that *they're* the ones that die. So instead, he falls in love.

And love resolves his doubts and wraps him in the mantle of its own protection. He is not alone. He is not alone. That isolated helplessness, that loneliness, is gone. And the fear. And much of the indecisiveness. His boundaries are not closed, no longer hedging him and imprisoning him in cold aloneness. He is more than himself. He is himself *and* his beloved. They are two, but they are not two, they are one. Each is to the other what he himself lacks in completeness, and the sweetness of it is that together they are such a comfort.

No more doubts about life's directions, career choices, ethics, sexuality. And no more anxiety over his incompleteness. He is more than complete. He is two is one is two. So he can throw himself with new vigor into the world and deal with the problems it poses. And if those problems are opposition, so much the better. With the recognition of that love and the strength of the union, there comes the next step: commitment in marriage. If, now, there is the opposition of parents, it is not a threat but a challenge. And how easy to overcome them when it is in the name of love! The opposition just makes the love much firmer, the apparent commitment stronger. The very act of opposing other people assures us of our own boundaries. If those boundaries feel more secure because of the love and the marriage that is so near, doesn't that mean it's all real? Doesn't that prove it's love? That it's good? That it will last? ("I don't give a shit about my parents or yours. We're not gonna let them fuck us over any more!") Doesn't it prove something that we can stand together and fight the whole world? Doesn't it? Doesn't it?

Well, no. Of course, it's nice to get things settled. But resolving the question of uncertainty in one's individuality and one's capacity to make it alone by tieing up with another uncertain soul may make for an apparently purposeful union, while the real issue goes underground. Smoothed over and hidden until another natural crisis brings it up again, frequently with disastrous results for the marriage that has meanwhile formed over it. When the school work is over and a new career must be entered, *that* may be the focal point for a new questioning. Or major changes in the course or direction of work can bring it up. Or the birth of a child. Or the death of a parent. Suddenly, it's there again. Who am I? Where am I going? And the anxiety of death. This time, with experience and perhaps growth, the outcome *can* be a firmer commitment to the self. Maybe now that he is older he need not feel so uncertain and weak while bearing his anxiety. He may even sense his own strength and competence. Delighting even in the pain of his aloneness, and disappointed that love has been no true guard against reality and against death, he may look at the partner with whom he has shared this flight from death and from life, and suddenly realize that their voyages need not be made together. Then, unless their building of a life has been somehow strong despite the handicap of a false start, the whole structure of a marriage comes tumbling down. And we have one more statistic.

That's just about the way things went for Madeleine, the beautiful and talented musician whom we met briefly at the beginning of the last chapter. She married at the end of high school, in the midst of attempting to resolve important conflicts within her self and with her family. Robert, her husband, was also very young. It was their first complete sexual experience which began their movement toward marriage. At the time they felt that it was love. Five years later, when both of them were a little more sure of themselves, they were sorry. And the marriage dissolved.

Now Madeleine is living with a young artist. She's more hesitant about committing herself this time, partly because of her experience and because she knows, on the basis of it, that she still has work to do on her commitment to herself.

Or she knows it because of the way she responds now to Jeffrey, in her new relationship. When Jeff's friend Don dropped in, Madeleine felt herself unusually threatened by the closeness of the two men. And she was made uncomfortable both by the style and by the intensity of her own response, the anger which she felt but could not express except by withdrawal into herself, into a tight round ball, knotted in her inner being—and in the throbbing pain in her head.

To Madeleine, still uncertain about her own integrity, still in the process of firming up her personal boundaries, the limits surrounding herself and Jeffrey in *their* relationship remain hazy and shifting. Partly, it's that she hasn't been able to commit herself to that loving. Partly, it's that, in spite of herself, she has committed too much. She hasn't committed herself and so maintains a more acute sense of her aloneness. Yet she cares so much that when a friend of her lover moves in to monopolize his time, the whole relationship feels lost to her. She feels the suddenness of the rift between herself and Jeffrey and withdraws to her own aloneness, unable to reach out, to touch one or both of the men. For her, that threat to what she shares with her lover, which seems so minimal to us, is met as a threat to her inner self. So Madeleine meets the threat with anger and withdrawal into herself. And it's part of her unique style that she can't even express it, nor can she, by herself, overcome it and let someone know of her need. It is not the response of anger which is the problem for her. Anger, as we shall see, is a useful and adaptive response in the process of trying to work out the issues of one's personal boundaries. The far greater problem is the very uncertainty and anxiety she experiences in the absence of an ability to be angry, an uncertainty that continues as she struggles to define herself.

Madeleine says it this way: "Sometimes I do get mad. Usually it's about some little thing that's happened. Something that doesn't seem important at all later on. And then I'm even sorrier. But mostly I kind of pull into myself. And when I'm there, inside, I get all confused and even seem to lose who I am. Like that night with Don and Jeffrey, I felt like I didn't even know who or what I was."

For Madeleine and others equally uncertain about their own boundaries, loving may not only be a threat to that developing identity; it may, by easing those boundaries to allow the loving relationship to happen at all, so disturb the sense of selfhood that it feels momentarily as if it had been lost. For them, the loss of control over the boundaries of their inner selves means a loss of their sense of personal identity. And the love they accept is a kind of compromise, a love that promises to make up for their inability to define themselves. Unfortunately, the promise is very hard to keep and the act of defining another, supplying him with controls he lacks and feels he needs, says more about power and domination than it does about the freedom that love can be.

Where love is *not* a flight from oneself, where it *is* based on honesty, on the integrity required to make commitments, it involves a confrontation with the threat to one's sense of who he is. It is, after all, the regressive experience of loosening the boundaries of intimate space to let another in. While we like to think of "falling in love" as pleasure, that is only half the experience. Yes, there is pleasure, but there is also the painful anxiety that we experience whenever there is a shift into or out of those boundaries; whenever there is a falling away of defenses. Permitting someone entry through those defenses, accepting someone inside, to loving, means enduring that anxiety as well. It means permitting the anxiety to remain in awareness without running, without becoming overwhelmed, without instantly raising new barriers. It means feeling what it's like to go crazy. And, quite frequently, it means to act a little crazy too. More than just in the experience of losing control. It is a little like madness and a bit of exaltation to love.

In most of what I've been saying thus far, the focus has been on the experience and responses of one person, a child growing up, an adult falling in love. But loving takes two. And it's important to remember that, even when only one viewpoint can be taken at a time, what we really need to try to see is the way things appear to each of the lovers at the same instant.

Each lover faces a stranger and brings to that meeting his own sense of feeling at one with himself, his inner well-being. As the strangers become lovers, whether gradually or in an instant, they each experience the opening of their own boundaries; they each can feel the openness, the vulnerability of the other, the fear of closeness and the wish for coming even closer. And with effort and fortune they do. And are taken into each other's emotional space. In becoming internalized, the lover is extended the good feelings which are already there, part of the loving which each one maintains for himself. Loving this new and separate person resembles the love for the first person to enter one's life, the love for mother which also was extended from the self and the love of one's own body. But there are significant differences.

This beloved person has been a stranger, and in many ways continues to be a stranger. This lover is someone who has been separate from you. Separate from your emotional space and from the body that is so important a part of that space. *Unlike* mother, whom you once viewed as a part of you.

As a separate and new person, the lover has his own qualities, his own good inner feelings of self-love. Those feelings combine with your own loving ones to create an impression of inner expansion, a sense of exaltation, a sense of being more than before.

That's what produces that roseate glow about everything. To walk three inches above the ground. Look out at the world through two sets of eyes, living a life that's multiplied by two, changing time and space as in a dream of fulfillment, of overcoming aloneness. That is it, of course. The mystery of joining together with some other, a separate and good and true person, so that you are intact, he is intact, and the two of you are even more of a beautiful and working thing together than you could expect from the simple addition of one and one makes two. You are a living part of a new entity; and you still retain what is you. But there is no longer that acute sense of limitation in being yourself, alone, which lies just beneath the surface of everyday feeling. You are there. Awareness of your body is there, heightened awareness. But somehow awareness of self as finite, self as mortal, that awareness is dimmed, for the moment.

Love is a binding up of the mortal wound of individuality. And briefly, for a moment or two, it can stop the pain of anxiety. So what does it matter if the cure is short-lived, if the sickness recurs? It's still worthwhile. It's such an exhilarating and liberated feeling. To be free at last of one's own limitations. What a burden is lifted! What omnipotence is granted! What strength for dealing with the world! So if it's all a little crazy, so if it's based on a shared fantasy, a delusion perhaps, upon a fragmentary grasp of the world, you'd have to be *really* nuts to pass up the chance.

The thing is, once you're there, you'd like it to go on forever. Literally. Unchanging. Forever. And it can't, because of two elements of adult loving that are intrinsic to it all, that make it possible in the first place: separation and sexuality.

Lovers love that unique difference possessed in each of them. Each lover's separate inner core of what he is and loves about himself. The two separate identities coalesce to create what is between them. But as separate beings the lovers take each other into their personal boundaries along with a far greater expectation of anxiety, knowing as they do that separation is inevitable. That is the irreducible fact of adult life. Even if its acceptance comes about only at the end of that life, through death, separation must come to us all. Or along the route, at every stage of growth and personal change, separation is inevitable, and with it some shift in the closeness of lovers, some change in their boundaries for each other.

There's no way for adults to beat that separateness. Children try. Children may deny it, fantasy or fight it, but for grownups there's no possibility that you can fool all of yourself, all of the time. So you're left knowing that love has its limits just as surely as *you* do.

Separateness and its accompanying anxiety are part of the price adults pay for the *possibility* of loving. Separateness is what makes sexuality happen and what keeps it alive and happening.

For adult sexuality to exist, the separateness of the lovers must be protected. For love to exist, the separateness must be violated. So it goes. An endless paradox, shifting and flowing back and forth, rolling and rising rhythmically to a fall. A dialectic. Or nothing at all.

The sexuality of adults requires distance in its beginnings, as strangers meet; and distance in its continued being, a space between lovers that remains to be crossed. While for children it is just the reverse. Childhood sexuality is the body-centered concomitant of closeness, a closeness that already exists in the loving of mother and child. And the child's love for his mother arises as an extension of the sexuality he possesses in the delight in his bodily activities and as an outgrowth of his inability to see her as distinct from himself.

When we meet as adults, we begin as anxious strangers. The anxiety has grown with us from childhood, from the threat to our selves posed by each potential loss of love. Now as adults we have become the unique person we are because of our life experience and the separations already endured. We enter the possibility of sexual loving, hopefully, with a sense of feeling good about ourselves, self-loving. But it is not as it was when we shared our love with mother. We *know* now that we are alone. And different.

The differences nurtured in the space between the lovers serve as a start to the love they will share and a spur to the conflicts they will agonize over. The differences of their bodies. Of textures, shapes. The differences of their minds. Of attitudes, ideas, beliefs. The differences of their style of being, ways of doing and seeing. Differences of outlook on the world. The differences between the lovers are a source of wonderment, of curiosity. And of the joy that comes from knowing another and being known.

For we want to know this other, this different person, know him in all his possibilities. As lovers we reach across to each other, often with words, trying to build a common sharing, a shared understanding, giving each other as hostages our deepest feelings and beliefs. But not at the beginning. The hostages are exchanged when the truce is arranged. We begin often enough in contention.

We've already explored the anxiety of encounter, seen the fear for what it was, some ancient memory, a preparation for a battle that never really comes. But the body makes ready for it. The nerves and muscles quicken and the blood is thinned.

We meet as lovers and there's the anxiety of meeting, the fear of what we'll suffer as we move toward closeness, toward letting someone past our boundaries. And from our anxiety we test that someone in mock combat. We want agreement. We want loving. We want merging and union with another. But passion doesn't come from simple agreement. The excitement of adult sexuality is generated when two people agree to disagree. So we spar, testing each other out, creating a challenge that dares each to cross to the other's territory.

Abe Burrows used to tell a story that made the point. It seems when Noah was commanded to build the Ark he was told to collect just two of everything, every kind of plant and animal, fish and fowl. He did what he was told and on board came a long row of the animals, two by two: two elephants, two tigers, two dogs, two cats, two giraffes, two zebras, and on and on. Once he'd got them all on board he assembled the multitude and told them how they would be there the entire forty days and nights of the flood and afterward they were to repopulate the earth. But for now, since it was already crowded, he wanted no fraternizing. So forty days and nights passed and the flood came and went. The waters receded and Noah started to let the animals off the Ark. Off they went, two by two, just as before. Two elephants, two tigers, two dogs, two cats, six kittens, two giraffes. . . . "Wait a minute," says Noah, doing a classic double-take. "What's all this?" And the big papa cat looks up at him all smiles and says, "I bet you thought we was *fightin'*, didn't you?"

We use the tension, heightened in the conflict. It's that

energy we use to take the risk of touching one another's bodies. Of risking that we've been mistaken, that someone will say, "I didn't mean that at all." And destroy our hopes. So our hearts are pounding and we reach. First with eyes to bridge the gap. Affirming and delighting in the things we see. And then, only after, reaching tentatively with hands to feel the texture of each other's bodies, then with more assurance, seeking after shapes and forms that give pleasure to the touched and to the one who touches. Seeking after guideposts, charting the unfamiliar territory of our lover's body. Strange smells and unknown sensations that we want to make a part of our carnal knowledge. To know one another, that well-chosen phrase of the Bible; finally to penetrate deeply into each other's flesh, an interpenetration, and through that joining of the genitals strive to lose ourselves in each other.

It is through their exploration of each other's bodies in sexual involvement that adult lovers come to know just what caress, what touch, what rhythm, and what pressure can bring each one to the acme of his pleasure. And everywhere along the line to that orgasmic pinnacle they learn to understand the language of each other's bodies, the ways in which they tell each other of their needs and wishes with all the means of communicating at their disposal. Not just everyday speech. But through behavior and movements for which there are no words. Or in moments when a word despoils the purity of silence.

They learn about each other's characters, their wishes and their fears, their style of making a request, rejecting a demand, their manner of presentation in the most naked sense. They search to find the secret of each other's inner being, the secret of their bodies hidden from others by the barriers of defense. To find those secrets, the wellsprings of loving, to nurture them and add a new loving in the form of pleasure given and pleasure taken.

And when new life is a possible outcome, when they want and are able to create children through their bodily pleasures, the giving and exploring is made larger, given greater significance by the presence, alongside the mystery of sex, of that other mystery, of life's creation.

The sexuality of adults demands that distance and separateness between lovers be maintained in order to provide the tension that makes the joining of bodies possible and desirable. We seek and continue to strive after that which is different from us, that which is not us, finding pain and pleasure in the mystery that divides us. And we use that tension to flame our ardor. And when we join our bodies it's as if the heat we create can melt down all the differences, fusing us as one.

The sexuality of adults, no matter how it is entered, whether boldly or shyly, is at first a fragile joining, a thin strand, allowing lovers to find one another. But the strand becomes a thick entwinement when the lovers use it to find themselves as well. When they learn from their bodies' loving that they have found someone who understands, who accepts, and who gives them back a vision of themselves they had only *hoped* to find.

That begins in the body, in the triumph of fulfillment, of realizing the fullest pleasure with another, of wanting to give everything, of yielding and taking in the same instant. The sudden acceptance of oneself.

Here is this other person, once a stranger. And you've given yourself up to him and he to you. And yet, though the barriers for once are down, and you have opened up your intimate and personal space, there is nothing lost. You give everything; yet you are filled up, there is more to give than you dreamed. And you want to give more. Give all. And your only sadness is the knowledge of your human frailty, the limitations that you know are yours, the knowledge that you're finite after all, but forgiven even your mortality in your lover's arms.

He knows you now. And you know him. You've touched his body as deeply as it can be touched. You've uncovered your nakedness, your body, in its imperfections. And you find that now it works. It *is* imperfect, flawed as a body will be. But he accepts it. Delights in it. Enjoys the very qualities you've always strained to hide. And you know that it suits him, as his body, with its human shortcomings, suits you. So you learn to love your body a little more. And his for giving yours back to you.

So you begin to feel at one with this other, this person who discovers you to yourself and who lets you discover him. And you want him to know your every weakness, every falsehood and transgression. You want to let him into the painful places of your emotional space just as he wants you there in his. To try to accept those human failings too. As if, by sharing all the hurt with this one person, you can end the painful guardedness that has kept you apart from others, alone in your inner difference. As if by letting someone in so deeply past the boundaries to your emotional space, you can end once and for all the burden of maintaining those barriers.

Loving acts to remove the barriers, acts to open the boundaries. Loving seeks to efface the differences that separate lovers, and to create, instead, a unity. Not only the momentary unity of bodies which makes the sexual loving of adults possible, but a unity of the selves of lovers. A unity of attitude, a unity of ideas and of feelings, a unity of motive and desire. A unity that will restore a feeling of a former time, when there was no sense of separation, no sense of limitation, when there was love seemingly without end and satisfaction almost beyond need. A unity that gives the feeling of having your lover always, with you, beside you, inside your body, merged indistinguishably with your own.

In adult love we seek to re-establish that union, that early feeling of being at one with another, that is the model of our first love, the loving union of infancy, with mother.

And we sometimes accomplish it. Or nearly so. Through the sexual mingling of our bodies and through our conscious wish to open up to each other, become defenseless, and share the vulnerabilities that are our hostages to one another.

And in the next moment, when our bodies part, when our trust seems betrayed by one who knows so much, we are alone again, anxious in our individuality and separateness, eager not to lose that loving, frightened when we get it back that it will go again, or, even worse, that we will lose ourselves in chasing after it.

You've found this great love, a joining through the body and a trusting of another with the secrets of your soul. And suddenly, you look up and it's gone. The human flaws you loved your lover for grow gruesome large before your eyes, and you stare critically, watching those traits, those qualities so different from your own, tear up the fabric of the love itself, tear up what you had raised between you. And it's not love and trust you feel, but rage, defending you, attacking him, anything to get away, to have at least the old reliable comfort of your undisturbed self.

That's the way it goes for almost everyone who enters into a commitment to a loving that is meant to last, a deep involvement, or a marriage. And the fact that it happens at all creates confusion, misunderstanding. Where are all the happy-ever-afterings?

We've all been brought up on romance, from fairy tale to Hollywood epic. And the basis of the fantasy is the chase, the dream of finding love, of capturing the beloved's heart. That capture culminates the sport. But afterwards—not much poetry describes the actuality of afterwards—the chase completed, the rewards rewarded, you must live with it. Twenty-four hours a day. She's yours. He's yours. And that's it. Alone together in your Gothic abbey or your modern tarbox.

Oh, for the fantasy of romance to continue! To keep on forever, just in the chasing! It's such a terrific way to have all the joys of closeness, of involvement still to come. To have the pleasure of your body without failure, without disappointment. To maintain the distance in emotional space between your lover and yourself. To have the expectations and the glory, before you, elusive, just out of reach. All thrills. Without the dues to pay. The hassles to get into.

Instead you wake up in the messy reality of dealing with each other. And you're shocked. Where did this come from? How did my sweet loving thing turn into a fanged beast? Is this what I get for all my loving? Has my dream turned into nightmare? Is this what they mean when they say, "The honeymoon is over"? Or are the Mexicans cor-

rect in their old cynical adage: "Marriage is the only war
in which one sleeps with the enemy"?

Werner and Clarice woke up in their private nightmare
after only three months of marriage. Werner was the more
experienced, more sophisticated one. He was ten years older
than his wife, nearly forty, of European extraction, and he
had left behind him in a Balkan country an old marriage
and a child. He had experienced enough of the harsh
realities under the Fascists and later the Communists to
leave him with few illusions. But he still had hope. If
Werner was short on dreams, Clarice certainly had enough
for the two of them. She had spent her childhood in
Catholic boarding schools, virtually cloistered. And a reti-
cence and shyness kept her from finding someone to love
until her late twenties. When she met Werner, his Old
World charm and solidness completely overcame her hesita-
tions. Soon they realized they were in love and they
married.

It all seemed happy at first, standard story-book stuff.
Then Clarice began to feel Werner's cleverness as an attack
on her. She felt he must think her too stupid for his friends.
And she became frightened and angry and suspicious that
he would rapidly grow tired of her and leave. When he
went off on his periodic business trips, she considered hir-
ing a detective to find out if what she dreaded were true.

For his part, Werner had thought he'd learned enough
from his first marriage to handle almost any situation with
a woman. But Clarice's shifting moods, her sudden rages,
really got to him. He wasn't sure which of them was going
crazy, but he feared it might be himself if things didn't
change. But he hung on. Things did change. They got

worse—for no reason he could understand. Then they improved—from equally obscure causes. Then worse again. He felt Clarice was simply insecure, a spoiled and sheltered American girl who didn't know what growing up was all about. He'd try understanding. When that didn't work he'd shout. Or stomp out.

Gradually things did get better. To a point. Still, whenever they went to a cocktail party, say, at the home of one of his business associates, Clarice would watch him from the corner of her eyes. If he talked to a woman she would ask about it later. It got so that they worked out a little ritual to keep from fighting. In the cab coming home from a party, Clarice would ask him if he'd found the women attractive and Werner would slowly shake his head and say, "You were the most beautiful and interesting woman in the place." Then they could laugh and the tension would collapse.

Clarice and Werner found some use in their ritual game. A way back to their casualness. Not everyone is so lucky. And every newly established couple runs the same risk, the risk that their loving relationship will founder while they try to re-establish some new sense of personal boundaries.

The threat to the sense of individual self doesn't just vanish when love is established. Love does ease the anxiety of being alone, of being separate. And we do look for that sense of merging. And of being at one with another. The re-establishment in adult life of what we had as infants. But removing those boundaries to permit another to merge with oneself provokes the anxiety anew. This time it's the fear of losing oneself in the wish to give oneself completely.

It is a fear that emerges whenever there is some event or some quality of character in the loved one that brings home the truth of the ultimate separateness they endure. This loved person is still there all right, but separate and a stranger. It's not like mother, after all, not like that original merging, when it was possible to deny that there was any limit, any boundary, because mother was experienced as a part of the child's world from the first.

Here is this person; now you are married, or living together at any rate, and you've given him so much of yourself but he's still out there, capable of leaving, letting in the cold through the cracks between you. And you feel as if he'll take your gifts and go away. And you're sure you're going crazy. And you can't believe that anyone else ever faced such pain, such disappointment in his loving. And you're wondering who to talk to, how to make it all go back again, how to hide it from the world that gave its blessing.

What's at stake in all these changes is the very loving that you've treasured, the sexuality that has pleasured you. Again the issue of closeness is faced at your boundaries. You must find some new ways of being loving and close, being distant and sexual, being yourself and at one with your lover, and all at the same time.

In our culture women are at a particular disadvantage, under a particular vulnerability to the obvious signs of dislocation during the early stages of designing the style of loving closeness that will work. Chiefly because they have been taught to derive their identity from their loving involvements. Women learn to be a part of the lives of their men. And so, when they enter a marriage and begin their attempt to shape that new identity, they feel acutely the loss of all that was their former self, even if the loss is not much more than moving next door.

Inwardly the loss is always greater. It is the loss of all the familiar styles of being that make up one's defensive barriers to the world. Those barriers have had to serve for one, protect one, maintain a single person's individuality. Now they will have to do more. They will have to allow for the meaningful inclusion of another; they will have to help build a boundary that surrounds both lovers. That shift is what is central to the difficulty experienced by the couple as the waxing and waning of love, as abrupt alternations of feeling and desire. And a temptation to call it all crazy. And although the culture's pressures make the signs more obvious in women, men are also subject to the feeling of losing themselves. For them, however, when so much of their personal identity is derived from their work, there is less opportunity to express the discomfort. So it may come out in the little subtle ways we use to deal with conflicts that we cannot acknowledge. Like the jokes we tell about a new husband's being crowded out of his bathroom by his wife's wet stockings. That particular image of a woman's physical encroachment on the bathroom territory, taking something from the man, in the mere physicality of her presence, has become a cliché in Hollywood. All the film-maker has to do to project a sense of confusion, of a man's being crowded out of his sanctuary, is to show him bleary-eyed, flailing away helplessly, or enraged at his new wife's nylons dripping over the shower curtain. And he has established with one stroke that this is a man who is caught.

Of course lovers can struggle, try to make it different.

They do try—and sometimes sacrifice the sexuality of their loving in the process.

As adults we seek that loving union, we seek to smooth out all our differences, cause all the barriers to disappear. To become one with our lover. But when that space between us is at last made infinitesimal, when that closeness is maintained despite all obstacles, all costs, when the troubles of our separateness are carefully avoided, the implicit anger turned aside, we pay for it. That separateness, that anger, is the price of sexuality as we know it, the genital sexuality of adults.

Adult sexuality requires the existence of boundaries to make its presence felt. It requires a continuous renewal of the sense of being different from the other, strangers moving to become intimates only to realize their strangeness. When there are no differences the friction eases and the pain of being vulnerable diminishes. But there is nothing further to explore. There is instead a feeling of profound quiet, of being at one with the other in totality. A renewal of that first love of child and mother.

And like that early relationship, the sexual experience resumes the form it once held. It becomes diffuse, scattered all over the body's field. The pleasure of the total body. It is the pleasure of holding and being held, of touching and being touched, of smelling, tasting, and looking. But it is not specifically the strained, forceful, awesome pleasure that seeks its satisfaction finally in one body entering another, the pleasure of striving against one another, body to body, with muscles taut, heart racing, flesh engorged, and tissues moist until the final moment of eruption and release that is specifically the pleasure of the genitals.

The pleasure of the total body, whether in actual childhood or as re-created by a love that cannot bear the discontent of separation, does not demand orgasm for this satisfaction. Only the pleasure of constancy, the soothing slowness of being close in touch. Orgasm as produced in genital union is too narrow, too specialized, too final. In fact, it is too threatening. For climax is a clear end point, a moment of ultimate physical closeness, an almost-merging that in the next pulse beat gives over to parting.

As close to one another as lovers may come in their mutual pleasure, as united as they may feel through orgasm, they become separated by the aloneness of the experience. It is our own orgasm and not our lover's that we really feel and comprehend, though we may strain and try to wish it otherwise. And when it's over there is the inevitable, physical *coming apart*, the disengagement, bringing separateness back into bed. And the sadness mixed with the joy.

When the need for a love without conflict and pain removes so completely the boundaries that separate the emotional spaces of the lovers, there is restored that sexual pleasure of childhood in which genital sexuality, sexual intercourse, is but a small part. The pleasure of the genital remains, of course. It is still possible to have sexual relations. But from the avoidance of separation to the avoidance of orgasm is but a small step. And from there it is just a little jump to removing intercourse itself from its special place in human desires.

Sexual intercourse is submerged as one of the body's many delights. Just as once, in actual childhood, the pleasure of the genitals was a part of the total pleasure of the body. The excitement of the genitals was possible then, as now. Even sexual intercourse was possible in its rudiments, its simpler motions, but was rarely, if ever, experienced, simply because it had not yet acquired the intensely focal pleasure that it later assumed, in adulthood.

Gradually, in search of love, in the name of love, there is the giving up of the questing that is adult sexuality. There is only the quiet comfort, grinding down time.

The long-married couples who have taken this smooth path rarely complain of their marriage, even when they come for help about it. After all, they're happy with each other—a placid happiness. So why complain? After all, we've been conditioned by the media to assume that if a man and a woman are fighting, they're in trouble. Quarrels are a symptom of unhealth in marriage according to the prevailing pop-media cliché. So if there's no fighting, if it's really peaceful, really quiet, that's gotta be happy, right?

However, couples, when they come for help, know, like Carl and Betty, that they have a sexual problem. Often they know because they've stopped having sex at all.

Carl and Betty were the envy of their friends for their brightness and their affection toward each other. After ten years of marriage they still held hands. At parties they seemed unusually attentive to each other, occasionally prompting suggestive remarks by their acquaintances. In private they had little to say but agreed about everything. They acted very much as though they had taken the magazine-borne prescription for togetherness as the secret of marital success too much to heart. They were very reasonable people, discussed all the daily issues that needed discussion, decided everything jointly, apparently effortlessly, because each could almost anticipate the response of the other—and agree with it, of course.

In the sex department, as they put it, things had never been particularly great. From the wedding night. Both had been virgins, although Betty had the edge on Carl in experience. They met during orientation week of their college's freshman year and dated steadily. In her junior year Betty wanted to date other boys and they agreed to stop seeing each other. Betty dated a couple of fellows, and nearly went to bed with one of them. Carl was too shy and waited for Betty to come back. And she did, finally. Carl had always felt a little hurt by that year, a little resentful of Betty's sexual adventurism. Occasionally he would throw it up to her in the few minor arguments they had.

They tried to be understanding and reasonable about all their problems. But this one didn't respond to reason. And gradually, since the birth of their child three years earlier, there was less and less sex. No apparent reason. Just no great rush to jump into bed together. In fact, each was a little hesitant about going to bed at all. Each in his private fantasies thought of jumping into some other bed, of finding some other lover outside the marriage, but in practice they preferred to wait things out together. Meanwhile there was Carl's busy law practice and Betty's courses at the local university.

They wanted help now, because they were asking themselves and all the sources of wisdom they could find—the sex manuals, the heart-throb columns—"Is that all there is?" They were beautiful, all right. And bored with each other. And desperate.

Psychiatrists might describe the relationship that Betty

and Carl have worked out as symbiotic. Symbiosis, a term borrowed from the field of biology, refers to the living together in unity of two dissimilar kinds of organisms, usually to their mutual advantage, each supplying what the other needs, to make a stronger entity out of the combination than either had alone. For humans, too, it implies an inseparable union, but the disadvantages soon become obvious.

It's all about the wish for loving closeness, the restoration of that long-lost mother love. To keep it always, with no threat of separation, the lovers must forgo a bit of themselves. To fuse, they must avoid conflict. To keep the boundaries between them open always, the lovers must minimize whatever it is between them that keeps them separate, whatever it is that is different.

Each threat of separation must be warded off by bending someone's will; each possibility of conflict deflected by someone's altering his personality, someone's deforming his individuality to keep peace. One person stifling his wish to say something to his lover for fear it will hurt; a lover yielding his own interests in the interest of harmony.

Should the process of yielding up one's uniqueness, or one's will, continue to be carried on largely at one partner's expense, the result will be some alternate signal of the stress created, often in the form of certain symptoms, some clinically recognizable disorder of the individual or even of the relationship.

Feeling his distress, looking for help, the individual may acquire in the process a *new* set of labels for himself, diagnostic labels that describe his anxiety, his gastrointestinal upset, his overzealous heart, his vulnerable body, all as symptoms of neurosis. And, should he be so inclined, he may search for the origins of his difficulties everywhere—except in his own style of maintaining closeness at the cost of his own boundaries.

Or one of the pair may appear so much the "stronger," with the more determining will, the other so obviously "weaker," totally compliant, that clinicians would describe the relationship as sado-masochistic, not because there is an actual exchange of pain as a part of sexual pleasure, but because implicit in that old sexual variation is the theme of power, of the submission of a yielding will to a dominant demanding one.

But mostly the outcome is less dramatic, less obviously a distortion, an aberration. For many people the yielding that goes on within the relationship to maintain peace, to perpetuate closeness, is effected by their keeping large pieces of themselves invested elsewhere. For a woman, the investment may be in her children or, increasingly today, the pursuit of an independent career. For the man, the pull of work can become hypnotic. And children and careers may absorb the aggressive energy which is kept out of the marriage.

Carl's and Betty's marriage may represent an extreme, but, if so, it's probably not so far out on the continuum, not so very different from marriages we may all know, or share. Or from the adaptations which we have to work out to help us deal with the issues of our boundaries.

Like the busy executive who knows that when he comes home his wife will want his loving attentiveness. She has been home, confined to her own routine, performed like his to make their common life more possible. He has been in his work, his struggle with the world. When he gets home she will want him to be really there. For her. To share his thoughts. Her cares. And he will want to do so. Only not at once. He knows that he is not able to be there. That it takes him time to loosen the boundaries of his working self, to let go of all the noise still in his head, to "unwind" his other commitments. When he gets home from the office he is not immediately available. Able to accept her again into his space and to enter hers. So he delays his homecoming, stops at a bar for a "quick one," walks home on pleasant evenings, comes home to silently shower and change his clothes, until he *can be there*. Lest her need of him and his inability to respond become the start of bitterness and argument.

To some extent, of course, there must be a compromise of wills in any long-lasting involvement, if it *is* to last. Whether it's one of avowed lovers or a supposedly unemotional business partnership. All lasting ties tend toward the knot of symbiosis. A certain amount of yielding of oneself must go on. Especially in love. That is implicit in the opening of boundaries, in the acceptance of another into one's emotional space, in the restructuring of borders to surround the newly made couple.

But we are all naturally Indian givers. We give ourselves and we want us back. In the next moment we become aware of our separateness, even from the person we most closely love. Through the reality of our individual needs, our individual styles, our individual differences.

And that separateness is the source of pain and conflict. Those differences which we explore in loving excitement and which we momentarily obscure in the joining of our bodies are the very breeding ground of anger and dissension. And not just friendly, slightly miffed anger. But genuine full-grown hatred. Hatred of the kind that makes your hands clench white, with salt in your mouth and your teeth clamped tight and a knot in the pit of your stomach while your body shakes in the strain of holding back. Anger that makes your jaws ache to tear apart that other one, the one you loved only moments before.

It *is* only someone who *has* been so close whom we *can* so thoroughly hate. Hate him for his particular qualities. The things that were so much a part of the love just now put by. Was his awkward smile a signal of acceptance? It now becomes a mocking gape. Was her husky voice a breathing of seduction? Suddenly it's a graveled weapon. Did you admire his way of talking, his facile way of intellection? Now it's all just a slick evasion, a parlor trick of logic to keep him from facing your truth.

Only someone who's been loved is worth that much hating. He's been inside. He's seen so much, learned so much. Promised so much merely in the closeness. Promised by loving, by joining in that unity, to be there forever, always, at one with you.

The anger is the anger of betrayal. Of an implicit promise implicitly broken. Wherever there is separation after loving, there is anger, whether felt or not, denied or acknowledged, a little irritation or an all-out war. Anger at the very separateness. Anger at the other for leaving. Anger at oneself for being leavable. Anger is what makes the separation real. It says to both people, "You are different from me. You are not me. You are separate from me."

"Violence lends dignity to a loving man!" So says the wonderful madman hero of the movie *Morgan*. He is right. Anger in the midst of loving does two things. It helps people to recognize their separateness, to remember that although loving union has been theirs until that very moment, that angry moment, yet they are still separate beings, responsible for their own pleasure, their own happiness, their own lives, and, more, their own individual deaths. Dignity.

At the same time that it forces upon us the recognition of separation, anger makes the separateness happen. Anger builds the walls between people, raises up again the barriers of their emotional space. By causing each to withdraw a little, it reaffirms and re-establishes the space between, re-building the boundaries of each lover's ego, the membranes of each lover's sense of self. A painful sense of self. Separate and alone.

In childhood, it was exactly this feeling of painful awareness that stimulated the processes of development. As children we responded to the pain of separation from mother with fantasy, acting to change our inner world, or through anger, attempting to interact with and to change outer reality. Both responses helped us to cope with the pain; both ways of coping led to the building of these same boundaries of the self, boundaries which, while they helped us to endure the pain, widened the gap from mother, from loving union with her, moved us on to become the unique adults we are.

Now as adults we have to go through it again. And again. We try to re-establish that long-lost unity with another because we can remember that our best happiness was there within. And we succeed. We find someone. To love for himself as we love ourselves. And we join in the union of our bodies and the love that lets down those barriers. And re-create that openness between.

But it doesn't last. It must fail to fulfill all our demands of it. To some extent it is impossible to fulfill those demands, impossible to fulfill all the fantasies we bring from childhood and lay at our lover's lap. Mother couldn't. Though she came close. Our lover, an adult like ourselves, must certainly fail out of sheer humanness, sheer incapacity to match us breath for breath, stride for stride, dream for dream. Just as we must fail.

And once again renew our sense of separation, and our anger with it. And with separateness, the return again to us of our intact selves, we can reach out and start the cycle over. If we can dare to touch again a stranger, our lover.

3

After the Fall

WELL, AT LAST. The word is out. Love may be what we're all seeking. Union with another to re-create a time long lost. But the root of adult sexuality is not only love, or a way to love, or an experience of love. At the root of adult sexuality is anger.

Love makes the world go round. So they say. But hatred makes sex possible. Or at least the ability to tolerate and generate and accept responsibility for that hatred which accompanies separation. For without separation and distance there is staleness or quiet. But sexuality will die.

And separation means anger.

Well, if that's all the trouble is, let's just get rousing mad, and then jump into bed and have a good time.

Except it's not quite that simple.

For the most part we have refused to recognize that anger and separation *are* the price of adult sexuality. Countless popular journal articles have for years sold us all on the virtues of togetherness. Professionals have helped people to explain their sexual and marital difficulties as

91

communication problems or as problems of technical ignorance. Even that group of therapists and teachers who
have at least tried to get people tuned in to their bodies,
have somehow fostered the notion that what's to be found
there is a message of pure love.

The result is that only half the story is being told. And
people continue to search for new ways to get together, new
ways of communicating, new techniques for making sex
happen, new shortcuts of their own defense systems that
will help them to become more open.

And, at all costs, we deny our anger.

And *that* cost is very high indeed. It may cost us our
love. It may cost us our selves. To deny our anger may even
cost us our lives.

When we push our anger away from our awareness, it is
because we'd like, all of us, to have our cake and eat it
too. To have our closeness and our sexuality. Without anger.
Without separateness. We seek, instead, the erotic innocence of our Biblical forefather, Adam, before the Fall.
To go back, somehow, to that time which persists in all
our minds, when somehow everything was part of us and
we so pleasurably at one with another. A time when everything that was good, loving, and sexual, was in us—when
it *was* us; when hatred merely *happened* to us, without our
being in any way responsible for it.

That was our first love. And we were innocent. Innocent of the knowledge of ourselves and of our own anger.
Small wonder that we seek to return again and again to
such love or seek desperately to replace it. To return again
to an innocence that forgives, that covers over, that protects us and everyone from our anger.

Yet that's just the trouble. In running from our anger,

in refusing to accept our separate selves, we return to an innocence in which all is permissible, just as once we thought all was *possible* in our infant world. It's the kind of innocence of self and consequence that will condone— no, *justify*—even murder.

The playwright Arthur Miller elaborated precisely this theme of innocence leading to catastrophe in his much-criticized play *After the Fall*. Critics saw it as a *roman à clef*, a thinly disguised portrait of his marriage to Marilyn Monroe, and attacked it as too personal a revelation. Rather than accept the very human truths raised now to art.

After the Fall is a play written in the form of a confessional monologue, in which the audience is made privy to the memories of its hero, Quentin, a lawyer, wrestling to shake free of the ghosts of old betrayals in his life. "His career is a shambles, as he sees only his own egotism in it and no wider goal beyond himself. He's been through two marriages and is considering whether it's possible, whether it's desirable, even humanly decent for him to involve himself again." His first marriage ended in divorce when he began to feel his wife's unyielding certainty as a constant reproof to him. In his second marriage, the focus of the play, he has chosen a woman who is very different. Maggie is beautiful, adoring, unintellectual. Hers is the classic story of the poor girl turned pop-singer idol. And her sexuality is openly acknowledged. She doesn't hold back. Quentin remembers:

> I tell you, below this fog of tawdriness and vanity, there is a
> law in this disaster, and I saw it once as hard and as clear as

a statute. But I think I saw it . . . with some love. Or simply wonder, but not blame. It's . . . like my mother; so many of my thoughts of her degenerate into some crime; the truth is she was a light to me whenever it was dark. I loved that nut, and only love does make her real and mine. Or can one ever remember love? It's like trying to summon up the smell of roses in a cellar. You might see a rose, but never the perfume. And that's the truth of roses, isn't it?—the perfume?

For Quentin, Maggie's open sexuality is also the promise of love given freely, love given with no thought of future consequences.

QUENTIN: You know? . . . There's one word written on your forehead.

MAGGIE: What?

QUENTIN: Now.

MAGGIE: But what else is there?

QUENTIN: A future. And I've been carrying it around all my life, like a vase that must never be dropped. So you can't ever touch anybody, you see?

MAGGIE: But why can't you just hold it in one hand? . . . And touch with the other: I would never bother you, Quentin. Can't somebody just give you something? Like when you're thirsty. And you drink, and walk away. That's all.

QUENTIN: But what about you?

MAGGIE: Well . . . I would have what I gave.

QUENTIN: You're all love, aren't you?

MAGGIE: That's all I am: A person could die any minute, you know!

Maggie invites him to accept that sexual loving, with no strings, no pretense of her sexual innocence. And that love brings to Quentin the possibility of his *own* return to innocence, the innocence of irresponsibility.

QUENTIN: Innocent! Yes, that suddenly there was someone who would not club you to death with their innocence! . . . It's all laughable!

Laughable, because there was a catch to it. That he fulfill her every demand, made always in the name of that love.

At first demands are small. Reasonable. That he pledge fidelity. That he reassure her of her worth to him. Gradually her wants increase. He must manage her career. He must fire a musician whose stray laugh may have been directed at her; he must terminate a contract she somehow can't bring herself to fulfill. He must help to maintain her public image of the sex goddess. All, all in the name of love.

MAGGIE: That's all I mean. If I want something, you should ask yourself why, why does she want it, not why she shouldn't have it. That's why I don't smile; I feel I'm fighting all the time to make you *see*. You're like a little boy, you don't see the knives people hide. . . .

And finally she demands of him that he give up all his life to save hers, that he accept responsibility for seeing to it she doesn't destroy herself with the pills and the liquor that she uses to calm her own bad dreams.

That is when Quentin loses his innocence. And his wish for innocence. Implicitly, he has promised to fulfill all these demands. In his need for her. In his unwillingness or inability to say "no" to her. In his acceptance of her lie that she will love with no thought of return. He has promised to love without limit. The other side of innocence. And it is just as false as Maggie's own promise to love without demand.

QUENTIN: God's power is love without limit. But when a man dares reach for that . . . he is only reaching for power.

95

Whoever goes to save another with the lie of limitless love throws a shadow on the face of God. And God is what happened. God is what is; and whoever stands between another person and her truth is not a lover, he is—

And he tells Maggie that they have used one another.

QUENTIN: Yes, you. And I. "To live," we cried, and "now" we cried. And loved each other's innocence as though to love enough what was not there would cover up what was. But there is an angel, and night and day he brings back to us exactly what we want to lose. And no chemical can kill him, no blindness dark enough to make him lose the way; so you must love him, he keeps truth in the world. You eat those pills like power, but only what you've done will save you. If you could only say, "I have been cruel," this frightening room would open. If you could say, "I have been kicked around, but I have been just as inexcusably vicious to others, called my husband idiotic in public, I have been utterly selfish despite my generosity, I have been hurt by a long line of men but I have cooperated with my persecutors. . . ."

MAGGIE: Son of a bitch!

QUENTIN: "And I am full of hatred . . . I, Maggie, the sweet lover of all life—I hate the world!"

MAGGIE: Get out of here!

QUENTIN: "Hate women, hate men, hate all who will not grovel at my feet proclaiming my limitless love for ever and ever!"

(She spills a handful of pills into her palm. He speaks desperately, trying not physically to take the pills from her.)

Throw them in the sea; throw Death in the sea and drink your life instead, your rotten, betrayed, hateful mockery of a life. That power is death, Maggie! Do the hardest thing of all . . . see your own hatred, and live.

Her answer is another threat of death, and he turns, in the awareness of his rage and even of the wish that she should die. And she commits suicide. Afterward he asks,

> QUENTIN: Is the knowing all? To know and even happily, that we meet unblessed; not in some garden of wax fruit and painted trees, that lie of Eden, but after, after the Fall, after many, many deaths. Is the knowing all? . . . And the wish to kill is never killed, but with some gift of courage one may look into its face when it appears, and with a stroke of love—as to an idiot in the house—forgive it; again and again . . . forever!

The knowing could at least be a start. Knowing doesn't make life trouble-free. Far from it. But it does liberate it from false intensity, from misplaced seriousness, and, hopefully, from the genuine danger of insisting upon the impossible.

The life of Eden, of Arthur Miller's play, is that a sexual love can go on, forever, without limit, without pain, without anger. It's a lie from the moment we attempt it. And our persistent belief in it can only bring about that very rage of disappointment and betrayal from which we sought to escape in the first place.

Precisely because we seek such love, the sense of communion with another and the pleasure of our bodies, precisely because it is difficult to achieve even for a short time in our adult lives, are we the more prone to run from our own anger, avoid and evade it, disguise and displace it, and, in a thousand ways, create the very disappointment and injury that we most fear: to be left to our aloneness.

We deny our anger in the midst of loving in countless ways, endless distractions, innumerable self-deceptions, some quite everyday, others more exotic. We can invest ourselves in the satisfaction of our bodies, in an endless sexual pursuit which is designed to take us away from pain but which succeeds, finally, in eroding pleasure too. We can absorb ourselves *in* ourselves, and so avoid the hassles of engagement with another. And end by losing all that's meaningful. Or we can devote ourselves to so-called higher goals, divert our sexual energies to work, or to our children. And run the risk of losing all our adult loving, anesthetizing all our sexual possibilities. We can go on living lives of quiet desperation until we run out of strength and will.

And then, even when we stop, when we face each other finally, in our separate weary selves, demanding an end to our loving in our rituals of divorce, we still avoid the truth: that our hatred is ours, and each of us must bear his own burden in it. Instead we continue the game even after it's played out, in the seeking of revenge for our hurt.

Paul's new mistress isn't that much younger than his wife Greta. She's not even as good-looking. And by contrast with Greta's cool, patrician bearing, Meredith is a trifle vulgar, unfinished. It was one of those office scenes that is probably repeating itself daily in thousands of places. But to Paul it's special. And Meredith is special. Or she will be, for a while.

Paul married Greta in his last year of college, on the rebound. He'd been given the air by the girl who had first introduced him to sex and who had left him after a year to marry a dynamic young business entrepreneur. Paul was left with a sense of failure, of not measuring up. When Greta came along, her Yankee background and manner impressed him as a suitable compromise. In nine years of marriage they have traveled far. He recently became a junior partner in his firm. They have one child, a dog, two cars, and a good-sized mortgage. They give a number of parties and their friends think well of them. At home they hardly speak.

This past spring, as part of his new responsibilities, he was put in charge of supervising the new customers' men, one of whom turned out to be an attractive young woman, vibrant and challenging, Meredith. Over these last nine years, Paul has had three affairs, none lasting more than three months. And a number of "quickies." But this one is different. Or at least this time it feels different. For one thing, all the other affairs ended after Greta somehow "found out" and confronted him. He would drop the girl and come home contrite.

Paul is fairly certain this new affair is a real finding of himself at last. He feels confident, happy to get to work, productive when he's there. His whole outlook has improved. He and Meredith sometimes get together in her place during lunch. Her apartment is only ten minutes' walk from the office. Sometimes they enjoy an evening together or even a Saturday morning. At those times they often spend a long time just talking. That's the part that both like best—the sharing. It's such a good feeling to be with someone who understands, who doesn't judge all the time. It's so good it even makes sex seem to be unnecessary—though it's inevitable between them—but it is so good and true when it happens. Neither Paul nor Meredith can remember having such good sex with anyone else. Nor such honesty. About everything. Neither of them can remember listening so hard, trying so hard to be themselves, to explore someone else.

That's why Paul thinks it's special. He's even thinking about asking Greta for a divorce. If he can get up the courage.

And, although this affair is already six months old, Greta doesn't seem to "know" about it. Except that her ulcer is kicking up so badly her doctor is thinking of hospitalizing her.

Sexual adventures outside and especially *beside* marriage are a terrific way to avoid the direct responsibility and effect of the anger of commitment. There is anger in it, all right, but we don't have to share it with the person who helps us to generate it. Actually there is an intrinsic separation to an affair or for that matter to any sexual relationship that is not committed in *time*. And that goes for a quick pickup as well as for the longer, drawn-out affair.

Let's take a look at one end of the spectrum of relationships—that most finite of all, that between the prostitute and her John. In the first place, there's nothing "abnormal" about the relationship of prostitute and client, nothing "sick" or necessarily "neurotic" about it. And I will second a comment by Dr. John Schimmel and caution against the creation of any "instant psychopathology" in overdiagnosing to fit a moral demand.

Whatever the moral issues involved, it's worth remembering that prostitution has been with us for a long time, and has always served an important social function. Nowadays sex for hire may be a disappearing thing, especially for the young people of this generation, who are raising themselves in an "affluence" of sex. Their apparent open confirmation of sexual experience carries with it its own issues, some of which are reflected in the problems—and

the manner of solving those problems—of the older generation of males who were raised on sexual scarcity and who
do frequent prostitutes. These men tend to come from
the middle-class. They are not poor, but comfortably well-
off. They are married. Why do they do it?

It's interesting that the same question, turned around,
is on the tongue of every John, and each girl has invented
a set story to tell those brave and foolish enough to ask
her, "What's a girl like you doing this for?" There is the
money.

While it takes a certain notion of scarcity to place a
monetary value on sex in the first place, the money is an
essential element of limitation, bestowing a sense of safety
on the pair, making possible all that happens between them.

Money is impersonal. And in our society, in which it is
the medium of a contract, it insures a distance between
those who exchange it. Implicitly and explicitly, money
limits the obligations inherent in any relationship in which
it becomes a central element of what passes between the
participants. Money changes a voluntary association to one
that is "voluntary for hire." It walls off the door to future
time, sets a clear end point, extinguishes our fantasies of
permanence, in that it can be assumed that when the
money is gone, so is the relationship. In more strictly
voluntary relations, we assume that obligations can extend
over time, into a future, that our friends, our lovers, will
be there for us, to serve us well as we serve them well,
depending upon our characters and our styles of being.
Love for free may be limited by hidden reservations, may
be equally or even more exploitative, but it is rarely as
explicitly limited at the outset. The passing of money may
substitute for deep caring and involvement in each other's

lives. It does not preclude feelings: affection, sympathy, warmth, tenderness, kindness—all these are possible. But they are seldom obligatory, and they are limited to the duration of the contract, which may be an hour, or a night.

But that limit to the future does permit a freedom, the freedom of the immediate. It lets each one act out those fantasies of sexuality that they cannot, dare not experience in a loving relationship of long duration. For the man, whose act of paying gives him at least a sense of entitlement, this freedom can mean that "bizarre" sexual experiences are to take place. And though sexual behavior of truly sadistic and masochistic quality occurs occasionally, most prostitutes report that their customers want a sense of having been good lovers and that the experimental sex consists usually of a wish to have their penises sucked. "Somehow" these men can't bring themselves to involve their wives in their sexual wishes. *Here* they can indulge because "I'm paying for it."

The prostitute's use of the sexual experience is another matter. Prostitutes, in general, claim to avoid genuine sexual release with customers, or they admit to histories of difficulty with orgasm. Very often they are bisexual, with a consistent preference for a relationship with another woman. Having sex with a man, for money, is a way of touching a lot of bases at once. It serves as a cover for an inclination toward one's own sex that is difficult or impossible to acknowledge. It maintains a sexual contact with men that reinforces whatever sense of disappointment has been instrumental in propelling the girl to pursue this line of work. And the money gives her a sense of power, an angry sense of having won, after all, a sense of having "tricked" him, conned him out of it.

Money builds walls between the girl and her John that

are ordinarily built in voluntary liaisons by the spontaneous anger, the hostility, that two people generate as their relationship develops and their differences create friction. Over time that friction may grind their relationship down or it may sharpen its growth. But with money there is no need for anger and friction. And little growth. It's all built in. The money is a constant expression of a subtle anger which creates distance. For the girl, her anger in taking the money is best expressed later, in the arms of a lover, when she talks about her Johns, those anonymous ones in her life, her "tricks." The customers may sometimes be openly angry, get out of hand, but usually they are too busy enjoying themselves and expressing, in their very actions of giving money, time, and sexual engagement to a person "bought" for the occasion, the anger they feel for *their* wives and the other women in their lives with whom they cannot cope. And any open anger, whether it is over a dirty washbasin or the implicit mutual exploitation, is still limited, in duration, scope, and depth, by the responsibility they bear to each other. To meet, fuck, exchange money, part. Whatever fantasies are generated or wishes satisfied, whatever drama is enacted, the show closes with the final curtain and the two leave each other with no more extended responsibility toward each other than any actor and audience.

All of which should suggest that a very powerful aloneness is at the root of prostitution and that both the prostitute and the customer need the distance and the separation to make their sexual encounter possible.

The long-lasting affair has within it a similar safety of distance. There is always present the specter of time, the possible ending of it that can occur at any moment. Unfettered by the ties of children or the threat of alimony or the social loss divorce still poses for us, the lovers know they can both walk away, and they may even take pleasure in the possibilities of parting, dwelling deliciously on that terminal moment as a goad to seize the time they have. Knowing that things may end makes possible a special intensity, and a special tolerance—like the delight in the most simple signs of life that are the focused cravings of a dying man. Albert Einstein once explained the basic concept of relativity in terms of perspective. He said that the actual time in which a man kisses his girl or sits on a hot stove may be the same, but to that man's inner experience sitting on a hot stove lasts far longer. In a parallel sense the knowledge of the shortness of time, its limitation, prepares us to make the most of an experience, to maximize its beauties and minimize its discomforts.

By contrast, a committed relationship like marriage or "seriously" living together creates a tension by the very commitment made to it. It will go on. And that endurance becomes a sameness, a climate and a landscape that is unvarying.

Humans, we are often told, seek variety in their sexual lives. At least men do. Women have, up to now, had a different set of needs. So we have been told. So *they* have been told. The disparity moved an anonymous poet to write:

> Hoggymous, higgymous
> Men are polygamous
> Higgymous, hoggymous
> Women, monogamous

Of course, as we learn more about the needs of women from their own articulation and their own discoveries of sexual selves, there will be a different poetry. *Their* need for variety will emerge as well.

The enduring quality of committed loving, its lasting over time, can create a threat of sameness. And the sameness, the expectability, is another means of altering the distances of lovers, moving them too close to each other, eroding the sexuality through the very comfort of it. James Dickey writes, in *Deliverance*, of the wife of a man who is eagerly preparing for a trip in the woods, with his men friends, away from wives, "There was nothing wrong with his wife, except that she was normal, and she was his wife."

An affair does not have to be like that; it never has to bog down in the day-to-day, the small matters of everyday life, the laundry to be delivered, the rent check to be made out, the car to be repaired. And even the mundane can take on delightful significance when time is short. The foreknowledge of parting makes it all precious. And the issues of closeness and of anger can be largely avoided.

After all, the really serious quarrels hardly need arise. If your lover is demanding and you feel threatened, it's still easier to yield a point or two, knowing that the bending is only for the moment. You can overlook a lot that in a marriage would become a major fracas. And that contrast of affair and marriage is especially effective in the lover's feelings when the affair is, in fact, adulterous. The anger doesn't have to be expressed with your lover because your husband or your wife is so much the better target. After an afternoon of happy loving you can go home and, having given your spouse hell symbolically for a few hours while with another, you can do it some more, in person. Yes, the very fact of adultery is a criticism of your mate, a way of telling him or her off, but without the risk of a direct confrontation. Later, when you do go home, you find yourself provoking an argument, being more critical, in triumphant celebration of your separateness achieved in another's bed, still avoiding the things that angered you, that drove you there in the first place. The anger is a way of telegraphing what's really going on, a kind of backhand signal for engagement. But mostly its indirectness assures that it will be missed, it will become just another niggling quarrel, another rationalization you use to help you in your new love. And it's just a little better to make love to someone knowing that the act is in defiance of another someone, wife or husband.

So under cover of their finite time and an anger that is constantly deflected, two people create a very blissful loving, a sexual adventure that renews itself whenever they meet. *This* love is helped along, is able to be a greater closeness, by virtue of the presence of a husband or a wife somewhere else who takes the heat off. So there can be all kinds of consideration for each other, a deeply felt reaching out, two people trying to talk, really talk, to one another, two people trying to really *be* with each other. The kind of glory they have always dreamed about. But in the background is the other partner, spurned and turned into a target. And even further back is the reservation, the felt knowledge of "no strings attached," the very hidden clause that makes their beauty possible, which each one mentions only in passing, to taunt the other back to reassurance: he can leave should anything go seriously wrong.

These are the limits which envelop and protect us when we choose, like Paul, to avoid the pain and anger of one relationship by making our separation outside of it, inside another relationship. And later, those are the limits and reservations we invoke in the new one when things don't work, when all the casualness passes over imperceptibly to commitment. When slowly demands increase, made each upon the other, when the closeness becomes burdened with the anger of expectations unmet, with the anger of discovery that there are expectations and demands at all. Or else the anxiety of separation and its anger bring on those deformations of legitimate response in the great new love, and finally there comes a new sense of boredom and of sameness.

And one day we glance slowly over to our lover in the realization that nothing has really changed for us; the magic is gone and we are left the same. And we find him looking back with the same horrible truth in his eyes. And it's over.

So we leave, maybe resigned, maybe hurt, but still hopeful of a new true love that will really work. Or maybe the search changes, shifts a bit in direction. Disappointed with love and bewildered by the physical experience of sex, we go on now to look for sexual partners, not so much for lovers. Because we know, in our flight from ourselves, from our anger, that the trouble begins *afterward.* That as long as we can encapsulate what happens between us into those hours or minutes we spend in bed, that as long as we can spin out a sexual skein by changing partners, having new affairs, so long can we avoid the trouble intrinsic to our sexual paradise.

Of course, not all affairs end simply as *affairs.* Many affairs, adulterous or otherwise, become marriages in one degree or another. When they do, the lovers must face again the problems of serious commitment. They begin anew to experience the gamut of feelings involved in the working out of limits of new boundaries. And since they will have some experience with the problems, they may be more prepared than before to work on them. Although the need to work on them can come as quite a shock to those who think they've got it all wrapped up already.

When they do settle into the hard work of negotiating the limits, of dealing with the hassles, these couples will have the opportunity to create a really working, living, growing, sexual tie. An opportunity they can capitalize on to the extent that they do not run away from the anger which is a part of their loving. An opportunity that is available to any couple in any kind of relationship where commitment is possible.

What about the others? What happens when people elect, out of their anxiety, to pursue a series of sexual partners? Sex itself as pleasurable experience? What about transiency as opposed to commitment?

Here is a great way to attempt to deny anger, to avoid separation. By changing partners faster than the issues can emerge. And it's a great way to come right back to the very pain we seek to avoid. It's the paradox of the French proverb: The more things change, the more they remain the same.

When a heavily committed relationship seems to be too difficult or when there have been a series of disappointments, it's easy to grasp at having quickie affairs of no apparent depth. That feels like one good answer. Meets the needs of the body and breaks the cold of loneliness. One-night stands, quickie affairs, have an ideal starting point in the dating bar for people whose trip is basically heterosexual and in the gay bar for homosexuals. In either case the setting is perfect. And conducive. The *anxiety* of meeting, of making contact through defenses against real contact, of pushing up your walls against other people's barriers, must be quickly suppressed. And it is. In the glibness of bright staccato commentary that quickly displaces conversation, in the need to be high on something, and quickly, in the screaming urgency to enjoy yourself, in the greed that meets your senses at every turn, to run, grab, inspire, guzzle down all the people in the place, lest, God forbid, you let a good thing go by, and all at the agonizing slow-motion pace of conventions that call themselves "cool" and condemn in horror the slightest attempt to bring up the truth of everyone's desperation and terror. The fear of being rejected, being unselected, left alone, for a minute, a night, a lifetime, pulls the regulars in to make contact, any kind of contact, and rushes them out again, to score, in a bed, and run back quickly, to score again. Before it's all gone. All the sex, all the youth, all the appeal. And makes it certain that real contact, real breaking through to another human being, will be a very rare event. Instead, there is the feel, and sound, and, most of all, the look, that is important. For transiency depends best upon physical appearance. The visually attractive is the most desirable. And the easiest standard of comparison. And the quickest. The brief encounter works best with beautiful people because not only is skin-deep attractiveness appealing on its own terms but it adds the additional opportunity for inviting a crowd to bed, at least mentally. Some people enjoy a beautiful partner in the spirit of thinking, "How the others must envy me, seeing me with her (him)."

The hunger, the anxiety, the battle against the realization

of loneliness, all operate, together with the skin-consciousness of people-hunting locales, to maintain human interactions at a level of pure *narcissism*—at its extreme a self-love that permits contact without entrance. Even intimate physical contact is possible for people who assume this mode, but their boundaries are really closed. That is the essence of the narcissistic position—secure the boundaries tight, like a cloak, against any genuine intrusion by life and its possibilities and dangers. Within those limits, the self-loving has himself to love. All the frantic activity, posturing, posing, running, and catching does not alter the fact that the final sought-after-and-inevitably-lost object remains the person himself. Sexual behavior may go on. And does. Genital intertwinings between two or many more people at a time, but that's quickly over and just as quickly is the turn to start again, to find someone new who will bring another momentary relief. Of course, the actuality of the other person is ultimately unimportant, because there need be no investment in building something. That something is a relationship beyond oneself and one's own interest. And it takes a willingness to face the hassles, clean up the mess. It demands an awareness of another's need and another's own destiny.

A by-product of the commitment to oneself is a superficial cool, a control over disruptive feelings, an apparent lack of need for the expression of anger. In a narcissistic involvement, explosive and particularly repetitive quarrels and fighting can be the exception. Any hassling is a good reason to end things. More importantly, anger, however painful and disruptive it may be between people, however much it may be elemental to issues of closeness and the means of creating separateness and distance, is also a way of caring. To be angry, you have to be bothered. You have to give a damn and more. You have to let someone in at least as far as to be able to be disturbed. And so, being angry means you are aware of someone other than yourself. And that, for most happy narcissists, is too great a demand.

This is not intended to mean that narcissism protects one against the uncomfortable experience and potentially messy expression of anger. Far from it. Narcissists have a lot to do with anger. Only it goes underground. Their style consists of denying anger as a surface element of dealings with others, but anyone who has heard the hissed "Oh hello, dahling," of Hollywood studio people has no doubt that in between loving themselves narcissists have plenty of time and energy for detesting everyone else.

The thing about anger that is not expressed directly and in open confrontations between people who both care about each other and their relationship, enough to put themselves at risk, is that it oozes out anyway, at the pores. Hence these self-serving, self-loving types do not put their aggressions out front in such a way as to commit themselves to take any risk. Instead their anger is subtly expressed in the thousand little ways in which people can irritate one another, yet accept no responsibility for it. The suddenly forgotten name, the last or late-minute arrival, the excluding conversation, are but a few gambits available. Should anyone think to confront such a one with his thoughtlessness, he becomes the model of suffering innocence—"Who, me?"

I said earlier that we love another not because of some deficiency in ourselves, some feeling of self-hatred, or mental illness, but rather on the basis of self-love, self-sufficiency. We need to love others not because we are suffering from an illness, but to prevent an illness—the disruptive process that is the end result of loving oneself for too long and too well.

Michaelangelo Antonioni has drawn a portrait of the final outcome of the narcissistic position in his apocalyptic vision of modern man, *Blow-up*. The film begins with an intriguing experimental design: the modern version of yesterday's romantic hero, the creator, the artist. Today, his medium must be photography, the Instant Art of the Instant. Imbue him with that dedication to craft which has been taken for virtue in our culture heroes. Exclude all else. All human considerations. See what emerges. What comes of all this is a magnificent film that a few wrong-headed critics viewed as an apology for the "hip scene." Antonioni makes no apologies. His is an artistic statement, but it is also a deeply felt psychological insight. The photographer has become so used to objectifying all of his experience, so inured to turning humans into subjects for the lens, that even when he witnesses a murder his immediate urge is to photograph it. Thinking he has captured the killer on film, he tries to tell people about it. No one of his drug-using friends can take time to listen. When the films are stolen he goes back to the scene to recover his sense of the event, again with camera. Unable to recapture the experience, the photographer is at length in the middle of a field where a nearby mime troupe is playing an imaginary tennis game. As they invite him to retrieve a fantasied lost ball, he is beginning to doubt all of his thinking. He is lost.

The moral, if it can be taken for one, is clear. A man who invests his energy in himself, even in the name of society's highest good, of Art, to the exclusion of other human beings and other human feelings, loses his capacity to know others (and let them know him), to know life (or death), and, finally, ceases to have meaning, even for himself. Call this last, madness. Or suicide. Or simply a vanishment as into one dot in a blow-up of a landscape. It is all one.

It is the ultimate consequence of the retreat to the self—the failure to love and to hate another.

Art is not life, but many of us have, in the course of our lives, tried the same escape route as Antonioni's photographer. Only less obviously, less apparently selfishly. Perhaps even with a posture of selflessness. Men have thrown themselves into their world of work and women have invested themselves in the home and the raising of children.

Earlier I mentioned the executive who comes home from his engagement with his business and needs time to unwind, time to sort out his mind, time to re-establish the boundaries of his relationship with a wife who has also been busy but who sees her business as integral to their relationship, while his energy at work is directed mainly elsewhere. That obvious disparity can be the starting point for many a painful argument over who is more invested, more contributory to the marriage.

Seen in perspective, both lovers can and often do make use of "naturally" occurring commitments outside their own relationship to create a useful separation within it. Work can be that kind of thing for men and for women. And children.

But when the involvement becomes exclusive in any direction, it will spell trouble. Men can and often do use their work as a way of avoiding the anger they feel in marriage. Somehow they find things to do at the office, or extra necessary assignments away from it, that take up all of their time and most of their energy. And the time for confrontation is precious little. Any moment that could be painful is deferred because "Can't you see I'm too busy?" Until things can be resolved only in explosive crisis or the rest of the relationship is whittled away. Not only is direct anger avoided, but sexual engagement is evaded when he says, "Not tonight, hon, I'm too tired."

Our culture, which is only now recovering slowly from its Puritan past and the high religious premium placed on work, supports this avenue of escape. People assume that work, by itself, is a good thing. Only in the little jokes we make about office widows does the truth come out. There, and in the desperate quiet in the dark.

Women, even more than men, have an avenue of commitment that disguises a narcissistic pursuit and an escape from the tangles of their adult sexual involvement. They bear children.

Couples who would try to hold together a relationship that is crumbling apart by having children should think again. Children are hardly a way to solidify a marriage that is already shaky. Far from it. In any marriage, even the most stable or workable, children *create* a stress. They do not remove one. Each new child becomes a natural means for creating a separation in the relationships within the family, if only by the fact that instead of two (or x) people, there are now three people (or x plus 1 people). And at its most simple level that means there's a whole new ball game, a whole new set of demands, a whole new integrity to be dealt with. There's the new and developing child. There's its involvement with mother (at first the most important involvement), its relationship with father, and its relationship with the entity that *was* and that continues

—the relationship of mother and father. If you follow the same logic for each family member—that is, each one involved with each other one individually *and* with the relationship of the other two—you can see that instead of the one involvement of the two lovers, and each one's investment in himself, the simple addition of a child creates nine involvements, nine boundaries to be worked out. Implicitly the old relationship is central, is important, remains to support all else. But that puts a strain on it. And from time to time strain becomes threat. And threat may be overwhelming for one or more of the people involved.

Without making more of it than that, we need to recognize that children may be wanted but they are a mixed blessing. In a family that is working hard to live and love and be alive, children are a source of the satisfaction of partaking in the mysteries of creation, but their advent, like that of the original experience of loving, creates a stress, a tension, makes a demand upon the boundaries of the parents (and on those of brothers and sisters already present), placing the issues of closeness and distance again in question. But this new loving is different. First of all, because the child, unlike a lover, doesn't go away. He stays, day after day—a reality that shocks many new parents. And a lover can at least return the love, and that makes up for a lot. As far as the child himself goes, it is, at first, a one-way proposition. He needs and accepts the love of his parents. He does not return that love in the same way in which it is given. He seems to take. And the satisfaction that parents derive comes at second hand, from participating in his growth, from sharing in his mastery of living, but, finally, from his own giving in parenthood to the next generation.

This last is truer for fathers than for mothers. For fathers, the mystery of creation remains an abstraction. A man loves a woman and in an overwhelming moment secretes a sperm whose union with the egg deep within her body is unseen. And the life which grows from that union remains unseen and a mystery for nine months. Yes, he can feel, through layers of flesh and fluid, the soft outlines of something, something definite, something moving, something alive and joyfully exciting. And finally, at the end of nine long months another moment of mystery arrives when she is ready. And he takes her someplace. To a hospital, to a place of strangers, where he gives her over to other hands. And the white-coats exclude him. And he waits, foolish and impotent, a victim of maternity waiting room jokes, to find out what they have made together. Small wonder if at the end of all that he has a gnawing doubt that the child he is called to see behind the nursery glass is even his.

Mother's is a vastly different story. She knows. Sometimes she knows from the first instant. Life is there within her, and a part of her own body. Or she knows from the changes in the normal currents of her body's flowing pattern. The alteration of her mood and outlook. And the slow swelling of her form. And then the baby moves, quickens to an independence, and its heart beat felt below hers, all these are with her in the certainty of preparation for the final moments when she is to bring forth new life to the world.

Those months of preparation are, of course, vital. In every way. For her health and the child's. And emotionally, the time gives her time to adapt. To alter the boundaries of her personal space, as they need to be, to make this mystery possible—that two human beings become three, that a woman can love and devote herself to her child.

Earlier (pp. 43-46) I said that the sexuality of mother and child is reciprocal, that mother derives from the relationship with her baby a sexual gratification, just as her baby does. But for her that satisfaction is merely a part of her sexual world—or it is largely suppressed. These sexual experiences begin when the relationship begins, while the child grows in mother's womb. It begins as a renewed investment of mother in her own body.

During most of her pregnancy a woman re-establishes the loving contact she had with her own body, that long-lost loving from her own experience of childhood, that sexual world of her own infancy. She experiences once again the diffuse pleasure of all the body that was hers in her own loving involvement with her own mother. She needs that satisfaction to prepare for the child, to nurture it within her body and later outside it. But that involvement takes her emotionally within her own bodily space, inward, away from the sexuality she has as an adult, with the man she loves, the child's father. To an extent. And so, to that extent, she is turned off to him, turned away, to herself, to her own body and its nurturance of another life.

And when the time has run its course, when there is the moment of birth, if she is conscious, awake, she experiences her own body and the child's in a sexual consciousness that cannot easily be repressed. That rhythmic thrusting from within and the responses her body makes to it have been compared by the psychologist Niles Newton to the actual experiences of sexual excitement in intercourse and orgasm. Dr. Newton lined up the data of Grantly Dick-Read describing natural childbirth alongside Kinsey's data on female orgasm and showed how remarkably similar were the two events as physiology. The Newtons (her husband is a professor of obstetrics) have made similar observations about breast feeding and sexual excitement. They conclude:

> Coitus, childbirth and lactation have common biological roles and they share at least three characteristics:
> 1. they are based on closely related neurohumoral reflexes;
> 2. they are sensitive to environmental stimuli, being easily inhibited in their early stages; and
> 3. they all, in certain circumstances, trigger caretaking.

It's a good thing for all of us that childbirth *is* a good thing. But the relationship of mother to her body and later *by extension* (as if she were repeating her own sexual growth with her own mother) to the body of her child *can* be too good a thing.

If you are a mother it's easy to find yourself so engrossed in the caretaking routine that everything else becomes secondary. And of course it is necessary that it does go that way for a while at the beginning of the child's life. But sometimes the centrality of the child continues, beyond the first three months, beyond the first year, beyond the child's own childhood. Somehow you get locked in, caught up in the child's universe, in which the sun revolves around *him*. Taking care of him becomes your quiet mission, just as his mission later will be to do great things for you, taking care of *you*.

It's another familiar theme of joke and novel, of pain and guilt buried beneath a child's skin till he can grow and seek the therapeutic couch that is to be his means for digging it all out.

From Niles Newton and Michael Newton, "Psychologic Aspects of Lactation." *New England Journal of Medicine*, Vol. 277 (November 30, 1967), pp. 1179–1188.

But though we've heard a lot about the child who comes from all this, the mama's boy, the angry pampered darling who can't seem to make the separative leap from her to love a stranger, we've not really heard from mother with a sympathetic ear. She deserves her time.

What moves her is a mixture of things. There is the sweet seductiveness of that involvement, a chance for her to maintain a love in closeness, never to face the anger and the pain of parting. That love she had once with her own mother, and somehow it escaped. Never quite to return in the grown-up world, the relationship with a husband or a lover, the demands, the sexuality. But now, with child, with the child as it grows outside her physical body but still engulfed in her emotional space, she has it back. And she holds tight to it. And tight to the child. Because the child frees her from the needs of facing the adult relationship and its messiness. And all in the name of motherhood.

So gradually the marriage that she has made becomes a shadow. And she may even leave her husband's bed, the better to hear her child's call.

As extreme as all this sounds and *is*, it's not really so uncommon. And in a measure it is a part of the reality of any family's life course. That for a time the central involvement will be the mother and her babe. The seductiveness of the tie is supported by the experiences of the body of the mother and the child. For her the interchangeability of adult sexuality in intercourse and the subsequent birth and breast feeding and the return to her of her investment in herself, make for a pressure that is later supported not only by the child's demands and his reality but by a culture which sees motherhood as only a good—until it's too late. Until our children come to tell their version of *Portnoy's*

Complaint. Or until we begin to question motherhood for reasons that have nothing to do with mother, alone by herself, but with the needs of the rest of the world for control of its space.

Earlier I mentioned that father's intrusion into the space surrounding mother and child was a mighty important lever, moving her to reassert her independent needs and her loyalty to the sexual world of adults. But when father doesn't make his assertions of himself felt, for fear of being selfish, for fear of argument, or simply because by then he too is busy elsewhere, there is a situation ripe for decay. And where mother cannot bear to tear herself away from her child's need of her, for fear of the pain of upsetting him, where she cannot bear to fully face her husband and his anger at her for leaving *him* in the first place, where she cannot, somehow, for a thousand reasons rationalized and psychologized away, deal with the separations implicit in adult sexuality, there grows the slow continued acquiescence in sharing the child's world and the gratifications of that world, a love that can be trained to remain, a will that can be molded to her own, and a soft, small body clinging in shy passion for her strong envelopment.

And the father goes about his business, elsewhere.

Surely it's not this way for everyone. But to the assertion that such things appear only in the casebooks of psychiatrists, are only the nightmares of the acknowledged "abnormal" patients, I must say: Isn't it strange that most people enter marriage in a heady mist of sensuality, in a sexual loving that seems to need restraint? And that so few of us can summon images of our parents even touching?

They lost their sexuality and the loving in the flight from each other. And so do we, engrossed in what we think of as unselfish duty, to work, to be a mother. Or engaged in what is much more obviously a self-serving means made into an end, the pursuit of *things*.

Things are intimately connected with the frail attempt to invest only in oneself, the sense of inner deficiency, that *is* the narcissistic position. *Things* as actual and material objects, or as abstractions, in terms of power, status, social position, fame. Things, after all, are reliable. More reliable, even, than children. *They* can *never* leave of their own accord. Most importantly, things don't talk back, don't criticize, don't, in fact, do much of anything, except reflect back the glory of their owner.

You can love things, but you can't make love *with* things.

Philip Slater writes in *The Pursuit of Loneliness* that if we can interpose a material object between every libidinal itch and its scratch our Gross National Product will reach its zenith.

He's saying that our economy and indeed our culture is geared to the devices which we use to avoid our grown-up sexuality and its implicit strain and struggle. Much has been made of our materialism, our affluence, our endless preoccupation with production, and our ever-escalating need for new means of consumption, largely in terms of economic theory. Social theorists who have talked about love and materialism have tended to place the emphasis on the marketplace first, the bedroom last. They see the deterioration of family life, of sensuality, of simple human warmth as the result of the technology and not the other way around.

Slater, for one, postulates that what made civilization possible in the first place, in the face of deprivation and natural poverty, was man's capacity and willingness to deny what was plentifully available to him, his body and all the satisfactions to be derived from it. He then used the energy which would otherwise have been directly expressed as sexual behavior to obtain the necessities of life. Gradually, according to this view, the gratification of the body was more and more delayed and the pursuit of material ends took on an eroticized quality that eventually drew to this end all or most of the sexual energy, leaving man as a creature more and more abstracted from himself, playing a highly complex symbolic game. The end of that game may once have been to provide life's material needs in order to preserve that life, in order to permit sex at all. In its evolved form the material pursuit *is* the game and the end of the game; sexual expression has assumed secondary importance.

I see it very differently. Man is quite capable of almost infinite delay of sexual expression. But unless man has undergone a remarkable change over the centuries, he did not need to make a sacrifice to pursue worldly concerns. We do not just defer sexuality, we actively run from it, because to accept its beauty means to accept its burden of pain too. In our running from ourselves, from our loving and our hating, we have devised a powerful economic machine that in our own time threatens us, and keeps us as its servant because its needs for consumers in a time of glut coincide with our own need for newer distractions, ever newer toys, newer means of temporary reassurance while we deny the loving that is our destiny.

W. H. Auden characterized the 1930s and 1940s as an *Age of Anxiety.* Today we live in an *Age of Narcissism.* Materialism is its economics and its religion. Hedonism is its philosophy. And transiency is its style of life. Andy Warhol captured the essence of that spirit when he promised a future in which everyone would get to be famous for ten minutes.

Unfortunately for us, our normal dilemma in loving is intensified in a culture which thrives on our deficiencies, real and imagined. While civilization may always have required the partial suppression of sexuality for society to go about its business, ours has a unique requirement that we channel our sexual energies elsewhere and that we be passive about doing it, that we be good consumers. To achieve this end, we capitalize on legitimate fears or invent false illnesses for which our technology has the only cure.

Children have always had to cope with their awareness of being alone and therefore powerless. In the past they could turn for hope of future strength to fantasy and to those myths that men have carried through the ages. That's what the stories our grandfathers told helped to do. Reassure us through their magic that not only was survival possible but so also was mastery. Now television sits where grandpa used to. Its manufactured fantasies fill the same void. Those cartoons of a small creature endlessly chased by a larger predator are aimed at the same uncertainties. And the endless triumph of the little one is reassuring. Only somehow those repeated over-violent victories are punctuated by a steady stream of products that are to grant the same strength to the child. Instantly. By eating the right breakfast cereal.

In the same way our youth are invited to a never-ending game of buying things to cover up deficiencies they are taught to sense in their growing bodies. Things which will clear up their pimples, get rid of frizzy hair, and make their breath kissing sweet.

"The unknown brings fear and once you instill fear you

can sell anything," says Morris Renek through one of his characters in the novel *Siam Miami.* By the time we're adults we've been taught for so long to feel the shame of having a body that we can be sold a never-ending supply of things to mask and hide the evidence, "those extra feelings, because you're a woman." The natural musk of our bodies is made ugly for us, and, instead, we are sold the distilled essences of other animals, or, better still, laboratory imitations, to be used as perfume. Perfect madness! To devalue the sexual product of one's own body and to be sold instead, and for the same purpose, the sex secretion of the body of another, less human form.

All of this killing of the body has its side effects. We've begun to feel our lifelessness. And that is where the new remedies, the new sexual technologists, come into play.

In a society so deliberately ignorant about sexuality there will always be a place for the new disseminator of the latest sexual "technique." And in our naïveté about sex we want to believe that learning some new skill is all that's necessary. That somehow a new how-to-do-it book will take us out of our dilemma.

The new sensualists and sexual technologists *are* performing a service. They are teaching ways to come into better contact with one's body. And in a culture which has pressed its participants to desensitize their bodies and divert its messages, that reawakening can be of enormous benefit in its own right.

But whether it's the sensitivity groups at one end or Masters and Johnson at the other, what they can hope to achieve is only a partial answer.

T-groups ask people to focus attention on the simple things, the stroking of a cat, the slow deliciousness of munching on an orange, the smell of fresh bread. Pleasures and sensations readily available to us at our bodily surface if we will just take the time. It's a way of reacquainting us with the sensual universe and our capacity to perceive it.

Masters and Johnson and the author of *The Sensuous Woman* take this one step further, directly into sexual experience. They ask us to take a step backward, away from the pressure of orgasmic end pleasure in sexual intercourse, away from the usual finality of adult sexuality. And back to the total bodily feeling, the sensuality of total bodily loving that is still with us from childhood but submerged. By taking the pressure away from performance and re-establishing that early diffusion of pleasure, they hope to promote a regrowth of sexuality, a relearning, with help and insight, a redevelopment of it from its earliest basis, the experience of the whole body. The idea is basically sound.

The development from total body sexuality to genital sexuality can indeed occur in adults if they will "do what comes naturally." The Masters and Johnson protocols insist that the lovers begin with continence, no sex at all. Each must explore the sensual universe of the other's body, at first avoiding contact with sexual areas. Gradually sexual contact is permitted, using the exploratory senses of looking, touching, smelling. But actual intercourse is still prohibited. Then, having mastered a rhythm and induced an exploration that is stimulating and gratifying in its own right, the lovers go on to complete sexual relations. "J" recommends intensive self-stimulation in many modes, but especially in masturbation, to the woman who would be "sensuous," meaning "sexually awake and responsive."

When people do come for help they complain of the obvious, their failed pleasure in the sex act itself. Their very insistence on reliable climactic pleasure belies the truth that there is trouble within their relationship and that their desperate use of and seeking after the pleasure of orgasm alone is another way of seeking to deny the messages that their bodies are sending about that relationship.

The technologists want to rebuild one important part of the total structure, the relationship of each lover to his own total bodily experience and to the total bodily experience of his lover. And that regrowing can bring love and sexuality back. For a time.

But even after the obstacles are removed, after ignorance is dispelled, after a new growth of sensuality is achieved and new patterns of excitement learned, there still remain the other parts of the involvement of the lovers. Here the emphasis on the body alone falls short.

For all they tell us about bodily wisdom and how to regrow it from its roots, the experts tell us little or nothing about the soil and its nutriments. The problem is that love brings closeness, which makes for sexuality but also diminishes the power of sexuality. Sexuality can be developed, but it can be maintained only at the cost of absolute closeness, only in the presence of separation. The answer to the dilemma lies in the acceptance of sexuality along with a dialectic of closeness and distance, a kind of dynamic tension within which a strong loving sexual relationship may grow. And that tension means that the lovers will experience and generate conflict, and anger and the pain of it.

Unless some attention is paid to that, to the interplay of forces moving people toward and away from one another in love, unless means are found for coping with anger as well as love, all the sex manuals, all the sex experts, sensitivity sessions, and sex therapy will not keep the painful beauty of sexual loving alive.

4

Till Death Us Do Part

O.K. IT LOOKS like we're stuck. No matter what we do we must suffer. Suffer our anger or the anger of those we love. Or suffer from the failure to deal with that anger.

Running away won't work. Innocence is a fraud. Arthur Miller told the sad and bitter truth that only the innocent can kill, those so convinced and convincing in denial of their anger that they no longer have any responsibility for it. The rest of us are saved from that by the guilt of our knowledge. We don't kill because we fear we can, because we're well acquainted with the murderer in our rage.

Sexual indulgence won't work. As appealing as it is to us as pleasure seekers, its leaning on the foundation of limits in time and expectation makes for a natural transitory quality. Whether you know at the beginning that there will be an ending, whether its pleasure sits on another, more painful loving, whether it's bought and paid for or merely traded as a fair exchange, it has all the virtues of that which remains as potential and which does not continue in development, fond dream, warm memory, but nothing more to change the person that you are any more than you want it to.

Self-investment won't work. You end up, when you have run to work or put your energy fully in your kids, with less than you started. You end up as alone and unloving really. And all the goods of this world that you gather cannot save you.

Unwilling to open yourself to the love and the anger you can share in sexual union with another, you are left with a love of self that leads to nowhere. And a mounting anger that goes everywhere. And in the end it comes to rest with you. Your hatred of yourself.

It seems, then, that no matter what, we have to deal with the anger.

"Is that all? Is the knowing all? . . ." as Quentin said. Surely, there has got to be a better answer in life than simply anger. Just the hassle of it all.

So far it sounds as if we've come this far only to learn that our dreams won't work. Our dreams of running from the burden of reality to the hope of fulfillment, to the fantasy of sex that is pleasure without pain, to the glory of success without risk, of riches without loss. And if we can't at least keep those dreams, what good is the reality?

What good is the knowing, then?

I can hear you saying, "If you're so goddamn smart, what are the answers that are better?"

You want Paradise and you want it now. I plan to offer you only this earth.

Not Eden and its lie of love unending, but this finite life of loving struggle.

We can have sex and love as adults, if we are willing to be separate from our lover, willing to deal with our separateness and not run from it. Willing to experience the anxiety of it and the anger with which we meet that anxiety.

Let's look a little closer at the separateness and the anger that accompanies it.

Remember what I said earlier in this book? The people I described were all trying to find and maintain a sexual loving and were finding instead disappointment and hurt. The issue central to their search and one they didn't understand, at first, was that each in his own way was dealing with the problem of delineating the boundaries of his own emotional space, within the boundaries of a larger entity, the boundaries of a relationship with another.

I mentioned the work of the naturalist Konrad Lorenz. Among the Chiclid fish, which he studied, the first concern in encounter between two potential mates is the aggressive one of establishing boundaries. To do that they square off against each other in full display of readiness for combat. When the two fish are of the same sex, one simply backs down and leaves the territory. Or they fight till there is injury or death. When it's two fish of the opposite sex, the same combative stances are assumed and then transformed into ritual, to postures indicative of aggression but in forms more suggestive of play. When the boundary question is resolved and the weaker fish (in Chiclids, the smaller female) acts out movements of surrender, the business of mating can go on.

But that doesn't settle the question of boundaries and of aggression for the Chiclid any more than it does for man. Periodically, the hostility rises again. And unless it can be directed against an "outsider," another fish, or transformed into combative rituals between the pair, the male will tear his lover to bits.

Lorenz makes the point that in species that do not form

some kind of bond of semi-permanent union, some kind of actual pairing off, there is little interaction, let alone fighting, between individuals. Instead there is just an anonymous crowd. The greatest amount of fighting is found in species whose social organization includes a pairing of individuals. Lorenz concluded that the bond between the couple is dependent on the aggression. It is formed from the aggression and, to maintain it, aggression is necessary. But the fish has learned to displace it "outside" or to transform it into ritual. We humans are not so clever as the fish. Nor so easily mollified.

We haven't, as a species, found suitable means for dealing with hostility. But one thing should be clear from all we've said. There's no getting away from it, no getting around it. Anger underlies our sexual loving, so we must, instead, go through it.

What does that mean? Well, the problem is not just the anger, though the anger is *felt* as the problem. The problem is the one of resolving our boundaries in sexual loving. Because boundaries arise in our life history to meet the threat of separation and, once we are grown, it is at the boundary to our emotional space that each separation is experienced.

If we want to understand how best to cope within our lives of loving, we can start by seeing what happens when the separation widens to a gulf and when that gulf becomes unbridgeable. When all is lost from that life, in death or in divorce. It doesn't matter which it is, because the issues to be played out are the same.

Once you take someone into your self, into your emotional space, to join with him in loving closeness, any serious change from that heaven is going to be a hell of its own kind. To let another in you've had to go through your anxieties, your protection against closeness. You've had to work to knit yourself together with your lover. The unraveling of the ties takes work too. So much work that it's really a crisis. Like the other normal crises of growth, this one is a crisis, simply, of separation.

First of all, in the terms we've been using all along, separation, whether by divorce or death—loss by any means—is going to mean a shift in the boundaries of one's emotional space. It means that that which has been taken in and made a part of one's emotional core will have to be let go, have to be given up. And that which has been extended partially beyond one's limits will have to be retrieved. All those elements of shared experience of loving and hating, the outcome of the resolutions that have been made a part of one's living substance, have to be let go. The good feeling we once felt in our lover's presence. And the bad. And even more than feeling. The kind and style of ordering of experience that our lover made possible and necessary are no longer to be a part of us.

(You once grumbled because you had to pick up his underwear left beneath the bed. Now your hands move automatically to the place and, coming up empty, are hurriedly clenched to your side.)

(Suddenly you're left to care for yourself. The breakfast doesn't make itself, the laundry is not automatically taken care of. And you have no one to blame for your unbalanced checkbook but yourself.)

The very way of looking at the world and seeing it, the ordering of experience, must change as part of it is given up. He (she) made up part of those things for you, and as you try and do them for yourself and by yourself, it's different and you're different. You're alone.

131

Suddenly you know you really hate Italian food, gradually you learn that you *do* like fish, slowly you will learn to like yourself, but slowly. It takes time.

And while the change is going on within you, your body learns it, plays it out, in its way of being in the world, communicating to others what it is. That is an important reason why it is so hard. Bodily patterns don't change easily and simply. But with the loss of someone whom we made a part of our selves, of our space, our bodies must change.

The subtle protective postures, closing-off, boundary postures we automatically assumed in a crowded room, that let others know we were one with our lover, those complex movements will be unnecessary and have to be undone.

And so you'll feel more awkward in a crowd. The gestures that signal attachment and commitment will have to be unlearned. You'll have to learn to say, "I'm free. I'm available. I'm interested," with your body's posture.

Here's a good example of what I mean by the body-posture signaling of attachment and availability. A young woman working at a military base in Europe told me how she easily distinguished the pretend bachelors from the genuine article. "If you're walking along, say into an elevator, and it's late and you're both feeling good and comfortable and suddenly he affectionately pats the bottom of your butt, you just know he's married!"

The years of intimacy set their pattern. These patterns shaped the motions of our bodies, reflected the important inner changes that the relationship had helped to bring about in us, the issues of our inner boundaries projected in the way we handle space outside, like the shadow images of a magic lantern. And when we seek to change them in our outer selves, we must at the same time forcefully alter that which is within.

To undergo this much change is frightening and it is risky. The April 1971 issue of *Psychiatric News*, a publication of the American Psychiatric Association, spelled out the meaning of separation in the dry statistics of mental hospital admissions for the divorced and separated. The largest number of psychiatric admissions occurred among this group. Before jumping to any further conclusions, we should note that admission to a mental hospital depends on many factors, all fitting together to lead to an actual event, entrance to a hospital. Admission may reflect simply the absence of family and friends, other people in the life of a person who can care for him outside the hospital, regardless of the degree of his "disturbance." And this one study is not exhaustive. I am willing to bet that if a study of *all* the potential life crises which can be viewed as separation and loosening of ties was attempted, the incidence of maladaptive response, including behavior that cries out for psychiatric attention, would be very high indeed. The crises of separation which I would include would range throughout the life experience: the starting of school, the physical development of the body, leaving home for work or college, entering marriage, starting a family, losing a loved one through death or divorce. These are just a few possible crises.

Let's stick with the experience of loss of a meaningful relationship with a mate. I do not want to create the impression that divorce is a cause of mental illness. Nor that it is the outcome of mental illness. ("George must be crazy to want to divorce me. That's it! He's crazy!") In fact, it may be the sanest action any two people can take in a long and unhappy life together.

However, the experiences and behaviors that accompany the separation process while it is going on, and when it is nominally over and done with in terms of legal rituals, are very likely to feel "crazy" to the participants. By "crazy" we usually mean out of control. And as we go about repairing our emotional fences, often alone and unaided by knowledge or past experience, as we undergo the massive inner shift of our boundaries that will at length be reflected in our presentation of ourselves to the world, we will be, we must inevitably be, "out of control," for a time at least. The unfortunate thing is that others outside of our experience, unknowing others, may overreact to the outward manifestations of our turmoil. *Their* alarms, set off at a wrong moment, may topple us from a delicate balance of struggling adaptation. And a false illness can become a real one. A momentary dysfunction may become a drawn-out disease. When all about you begin to doubt your sanity and you have already doubted it, the next step can be inside the institutional walls.

There is no normality in an abnormal situation. If you reacted to a major loss in life with genuine aplomb, that *would* be cause for worry. If you experienced the loss of someone, someone who has shared your life and loving, someone who has been within your personal space, and you were not a little crazy in response, *that* would be crazy.

Losing someone means *letting* go and, like the moment of encounter, of *coming together*, it means that there will be anxiety. For whether it is in opening ourselves up to let someone in, or in becoming vulnerable and open to let someone go, our boundaries must give way. The difference is that *letting* go is tougher. Because there has been a history of shared experience, there has been a reality of a life together. Meeting someone frightens through the *fantasy* of what can happen; losing that someone hurts through the need for reliving the *reality* of what has happened already.

What you've experienced together with your lover is past, but its effect remains with you, in the present, in your way of being, until you can sort it out and free yourself.

To find yourself again after a loss and to be free means that you will have to do the work of caring for your boundaries.

Olivia was 24 when she was suddenly deserted by her husband. It happened in Europe, where they had gone to live while he served in the military. The marriage had lasted two years. It had been a whirlwind courtship, and she had been swept up and off by Richard, the first and only man she had known. Before meeting him, Olivia had led a sheltered and pampered life as a debutante, occupying herself with charity work in the midwestern town where her socially prominent family ran things. She had never been in a position where she had to take care of herself. She had never had to make any decisions. Everything was decided for her by her mother. When Richard found her in the clinic she visited weekly, he quickly took over. He was a forceful, self-assured, almost cocky young man.

After two years of what seemed to be a happy marriage for both, Richard was inducted as an officer and the two set off on a European idyl. But it didn't turn out quite that way for her. Richard began to notice the attractive young women in the local cafes, and Olivia began to appear more and more drab and uninteresting. To him, her naïve charm became boring inexperience, and one day he announced that he wanted out of their marriage. He told her why, but he didn't have to. Her shortcomings were only too obvious to her. She had always thought herself scrawny and unattractive. Richard's early interest had been a happy surprise. Compliant as usual, Olivia agreed to let him go. She prepared herself to return home. It was while she was packing that things began to close in on her, that she began to feel strange feelings, that the panic mounted to the point where she needed help.

When the local authorities in charge of military families finally learned of her predicament and referred her to my clinic, she was in quite a state. It turned out that Olivia was in actuality a very talented and competent person, fully trained to work with children. That kind of skill was vitally needed for helping the children of other soldiers stationed abroad. But she had never held a real job before. Even before she could seriously think of work, of establishing herself in her own right, it was necessary for her to begin to deal with her feelings. First of all, she was petrified. For the first time in her life *she* was in charge. The entire responsibility was on her shoulders. To provide for herself. To take direction of her life. To make her own decisions in her own way. Freedom! Well, freedom is heady stuff, but not under these circumstances. She had thought of running home, where she would be safe, but the counterbalancing feelings of embarrassment caused her to feel that she must somehow use this crisis to shape her life differently. For the first time in her life she would have to master it, alone. From deciding when to go to sleep and what she would eat to negotiating travel from city to city in a foreign language. All this for a woman who had never been on a train by herself before!

Everyone who loses a mate feels exposed and alone. Olivia's terror and her vulnerability were exaggerated by the cloistered quality of her life, but the fear she felt, the momentary disorganization, differs only in degree from the experience of anyone who must suddenly start to live without the protective envelope of a relationship.

In that vulnerability of a loss you are suddenly confronted with your essential helplessness, not because you *are* helpless in life, or incompetent, or unattractive, or whatever it is that you imagine and use to flagellate yourself. But you are helpless in one important sense. You are helpless to stop the loss, helpless to stop the opening of your intimate space that losing a person from your life represents. Momentarily, that involuntary dissolution of your barriers brings back the feeling of life as it was when you were little and the caring grownups, mother and father, could leave you at their will, and, you felt, at their whim. And the knowledge of their leaving made you realize how truly frail you were, how much you needed them, how tenuous and fragile was your mastery of life. And now, grown-up and adequate to the degree that you have made yourself, you still cannot stem the tide, turn back time, or change another's heart. And the lover whom you've trusted and taken in can leave you feeling torn and open and alone and seemingly helpless. But—and this is a big "but"—not really helpless as an adult. For when you can recover the adult parts of yourself and put them in some semblance of together, you can go on and function. And maybe even better than before.

To do it you must pay some attention to the feelings of the child within. Feelings of all the times in your child life, in your life growing up, when you were faced with separation. And with love.

Our emotional space is fenced off by our emotions, grown and modified by feelings of loving and of hating. The loving feelings tend to open us, to dissolve for a time our barriers to others. The angry feelings close off the barriers to our inner selves. Loving is inclusive. It brings the whole world in, and it makes us a part of the world and the world a part of us, merged, indistinguishable. This is frightening in its own right. Hating, on the other hand, is exclusive. It reminds us of our limits, our integrity. It sets us apart from others and sets others apart from us.

It is primarily in the feelings of loving and of hating, and in the memories of experience which evoked those feelings, that we must deal when we seek to care for our boundaries. The caring process is not so much one of repair, or restitution, as it is a stocktaking, a look inward, a look at oneself, at the processes of our operating, the ways we have gone about becoming and being what we are. Caring for our boundaries is asking again the eternal question: *Who am I?*

We experience the operations of our being, we understand the processes that have made up our boundaries, by reliving our experiences of loss.

That is what makes doing it so difficult. Reliving those losses of our past, together with the all too painful one of our present, floods us with unwished-for feelings, most of them unpleasant. But it's unavoidable. We are blessed with memory, like it or not. Loss brings memory of loss. We can try to choose to use the experience and our memory of it in order to grow—or we can try to run away even from this reality.

One unfortunate tendency we all share as humans is our inclination to try to avoid what is real. We laugh at the ostrich putting its head in the sand when startled— and promptly do the same thing ourselves. We want to split our feelings up into neat packages. We want to love someone completely and entirely. If we hate somebody, we want that to be pure too. No troublesome admixtures of a little of this and a little of that. A neat trick we all use is to turn an experience of one feeling into its apparent opposite.

Suppose you are left by someone—someone with whom there has been time shared and a sense of caring. You experience the loss as happening *to* you. You are passive, the recipient of the bad news and bad feelings. How do you react? You get angry or hateful, assaultive or violent. Or all of these by turns. In an instant you know that he was really the worst person in the world, that bastard! That son of a bitch! Now you can be glad he's gone because he was a totally worthless human being anyway.

The point is that you have turned an essentially passive experience, that of being left, into an active one, that of being angry. You have converted a passive *action* into an active *emotion*. Or to put it more accurately, in being left you endured the world's acting on you (the world of your lover) and in hating back you begin to act upon the world. And in the interval of the quick change from passive being left to active hating, you need not experience the actual sense of loss, the pain and sadness of it. Your new feelings are saying for you, "Go to the devil. I never wanted you anyway. You are not *leaving* me. I'm throwing you out." So even though the anger creates a boundary between you and your lover, it does not establish any greater distance.

It has not helped you to actually separate, and in a complex sense it has brought you close. Anger is still caring, and caring is a tie.

Hating someone for leaving you is easy and natural as an initial response. It is, to be sure, a necessary response, as part of the process of closing the wound, restoring your integrity as a self. It makes you feel better for right now, but if that is all you can feel, if venom for a lost love is all you can muster, it will not do anything to help you become free of that love and it will not permit you to grow from the loss. Instead you may bog down in bitterness, preoccupied with energy-depleting schemes of vengeance, tied down in useless drawn-out battles.

Nor will the complementary response of loving sadness, by itself, gain you your freedom. It will not do to dwell only on fantasies of longing, yearning dreams of restitution, the magic wish that somehow time will turn around and make it right again. That somehow, you can, with a will and a struggle, bring your lover back. To see your lover lost as perfect, to keep on and only with the loving after it is truly gone, is useful only to the poetry of ballads. Carrying the torch beyond its lifetime is merely lighting up a house for haunting. True grieving exorcises ghosts.

To separate and re-establish your integrity solidly, you must experience the anger at losing someone important to your life. You must also endure the painful sadness of that loss, the yearning dream drawn out to its extinction. The realization that someone is truly gone. The anger rebuilds the walls, closes us off from intimacy. The sadness is the memory of loving experience of which the wall is made. Without the anger you do not let go of the other, of your lover. Anger casts him out from you and lets you know again you are not him, you are not two, you are you. Sadness is the feeling of the loving past, carried on into the present, letting you keep the knowledge of that love, giving you back the truth of yourself. Sadness is the letting go of love, and the acceptance of its death, but it keeps alive the ability to love. Anger erects our boundaries. Sadness puts the finishing touches to them, modulates the oppressiveness of them, convinces us finally of our integrity and our aloneness, and prepares us for entering the world again in search of someone else to love.

Here again is where the socially established rituals come heavily into play, helping us to handle things better in some ways, hindering us in others. We need the rituals of mourning and divorce to handle death and dissolution of a marriage because without them we might not know what to do. When we must give up someone who has been a part of our lives, we experience a kind of falling away of certainty, like an elevator moving too fast or the rollercoaster car descending from its apogee, and it moves us to cry out, "How come nobody told me it would be like this?" And that is a common reaction to it. Nobody was ever prepared for the moment of self-discovery. Of self-contact. Maybe because if you were prepared it wouldn't happen with the same effectiveness. You have to be running at full tilt when the mirror is suddenly flung across your path. And there you are.

The rituals of separation arise from the need to dispel doubt about how to be in a crisis, a time of change. One of the virtues of formalized marriage is that it gives social credibility to our dreams. Divorce is then a ritual of awakening. When the dream has not been fully realized, divorce is necessary to complete it, to actualize what is left as mere potential. The parting of divorce completes what is absent from the daily life of the marriage. One of the most common experiences of those engaged in the rituals of separating is their dialectic with their previous experience: Suddenly the meek are strong, the helpless made whole, and the powerful, meek. The divorce is like a chemical bath for the marriage, bringing out the elements heretofore hidden from view but present nevertheless.

When a divorce happens, the central actors in the ritual become swept up in forces that are of their own generating but not of their own control. Other figures—lawyers, judges, psychiatrists—enact powerful roles of influence. Divorce in our society is legally an adversary proceeding. That means that it can never come about by common agreement; it must, instead, be a public battle.

Someone must assume the role of the innocent; another someone must become the guilty. These lovers turned adversaries each have their separate champions, the attorneys. And a judge sits to represent the interests of society. The battle is over who will get the blame, or the spoils of some sort of victory, or whatever. Its actual content is immaterial. The lovers are given their prescribed lines to read, to satisfy their part in the ritual and the categories of the court. They must devise the "grounds" for divorce, reasons why the marriage doesn't work though they do not know themselves.

The really important contribution of the process of divorce, the court appearances and the mock combat of opposing lawyers, is to create the embattled atmosphere within which the two former lovers can square off and really express their anger at their loss. All the hassle, the harassment, and the wrangling which the working of divorce procedure generates serve this major end of giving channel and vent to the anger people feel at separation, which they cannot otherwise express. If, as is often true, the lovers never were this honest within the marriage, never could confront each other and express their rage, the rituals provide an opportunity, a means to complete the structure of the marriage by making actual what was latent in it.

And as awful as divorce fights are to endure, the rituals yet provide some safety, a way to express destructive feelings openly and to create hostile actions vicariously, through the actors of the drama, lawyers and judges. Without that safety there would likely be more homicides than divorces.

Lawyers often catalyze the fighting. (He's trying to cheat you out of what's rightfully yours. Let's ask the court for more money for support.") ("She's probably running around now having a good time with somebody. Let's hire a detective and get the goods on her.") But even so, even when they do generate pain, the long-term goal is toward what is the lovers' interest.

The entire process of legal ritual, with all its troubles and unpleasantness, provides a start for the very real and internal process of putting someone out of your life. In the setting of the lawyer's office the image of the person you have loved becomes much clearer. He is very different from you, with interests of his own, a future of his own to protect. You begin to feel separated in very concrete terms of dollars and cents, of privileges and responsibilities, spelled out and contracted.

Where our rituals fail us is in the carry-through. They are good for getting things started, for evoking anger to help us establish our separateness. But there are no provisions for ritualizing and giving expression to the sadness. That you must do alone, unprepared, with no one to write the script. Somewhere there needs to be provision for the sadness, some acknowledgment that the loss has been of something valued. Without that sadness, that acknowledgment, you really *do* lose a piece of value in yourself when it's all over. After all, if your lover is so worthless, how came it to be that you, discriminating and sensitive as you know yourself to be, placed such a faith in him in the first place? Without the sadness which confirms that value, the tie of anger holds you still and you are left separate but incomplete. Your ability to find yourself, to find someone else, remains somehow impaired.

Loss, the departure of a loved one from our emotional space, threatens us with loss of ourselves, much as love itself was such a threat. Remember that I pointed out just how loving someone is a threat to oneself, one's old self, one's old boundaries. And that the threat was met with defensive maneuvers from the moment of encounter. Sometimes the threat was met with a premature running into love, a premature commitment, when the sense of losing of oneself seemed overwhelming, as it often does in adolescence. Such faulty loving at the threat of losing oneself may later terminate in divorce.

With a loss, as in divorce, the threat is also felt as to the self, the sense of one's integrity. Because the shifting of one's boundaries, the changes of investment, may temporarily be felt as a depletion of all that has been loving and lovable within that inner space. This time, too, the threat and the anxiety are met with defenses, sometimes of premature commitment, but often enough of short-term loving.

Here is an important basis for the promiscuity that frequently follows divorce. The effort of the repeated episodes of loving that are quickly ended is in an important sense the regaining of the self. Promiscuity after loss should not be misinterpreted, as it often has been, as a sign of psychopathology. Rather it is a curious part of an attempt to heal. And it encapsulates within it a wide range of feeling states and defenses. It expresses anger at the mate who is gone. As in the words of Nelly Forbush, the nurse in the musical *South Pacific* who sang, "I'm Gonna Wash That Man Right Outa My Hair." It restates in shorthand the drama of the old love, its start and its end. And most importantly, it puts the person who has lost a love in touch again with his body.

For the newly divorced, promiscuity is an adaptive pattern, a way of exerting their sexual and personal independence, a means of reassuring themselves of attractiveness and sexual value, a symbolic means of expressing anger at one's spouse and indirectly at all men or women. And it is a way, albeit a potentially exacting way, of rediscovering oneself, one's body and its capacities, sensations, freedoms, through and with the bodies of others. Promiscuity in the newly divorced can be a very important means for re-establishing the boundaries, for re-creating his or her integrity.

In the sense of helping to recover and preserve the self, promiscuity at the end of marriage serves the same function as does premature marriage itself—the preservation of the boundaries of the self. This is not so astonishing when you recall that the threat is felt as very much the same, whether it results from the momentary dissolution of the boundaries as someone is taken in when loving starts, or the selfsame shifts in those emotional barriers when someone goes and loving dies.

But, basically, to recover yourself you must address yourself in loving to your lost love, even with the anger you truly feel.

That is the paradox of divorce and separation. To free yourself from an entanglement, to leave, you must recall and retain some of your loving for your lost love. Love for him loosens the tie and gives you back yourself. Often it can only happen afterward, after the madness and the stress of the rituals of anger have abated. By loving him in sad memory you retain for yourself your best elements and you can retrieve fully the investments you have made. And even more, you can grow in wisdom and in strength from the relationship. You then can make the best parts of that loving an active part of your new life alone. By loving him even after the anger of being left has been yours, you start to heal the wounds and then can function better than you did before you even started the relationship. By loving still, in spite of everything, you will have incorporated new strength to face the world, the elements you most admired in his character now making up a part of yours.

The loving frees you finally to seek out new styles of living, new ways of being and doing, a new wholeness. When the mourning is truly complete, energy is more available than it ever was. You find that you can do many more things. Things you never thought you could do before, ways of living with your body you had not imagined possible. From developing new tastes in clothes to trying out new athletic skills. The sadness of loving finishes the process begun in your anger and makes you separate as an adult.

What makes this paradox of separation in divorce and

death especially pertinent is its complementary relationship to another paradox—the one we have been examining
all along as the basis for sexual union in marriage or any
committed relationship. In divorce, anger is necessary to
begin the separation and loving makes it truly possible. In
a marriage, the loving begins the process of closeness and
sexuality. It is anger that provides the necessary separation
that makes the marriage relationship complete and whole
and maintains its sexual tension, from start to finish. If we
would truly let go of someone in divorce, we must call up
our love for him. If we want to maintain our sexual loving
in marriage, we have to learn to tolerate and trust our anger.

5

Violence Lends Dignity

In the midst of love comes anger, unavoidable, basic to its growth. In the best of love, in the greatest marriage, there will be and continue and recur, the fighting, the arguing—inevitable, unpredictable, except that it *will be.*

Mike is a television producer. Today he had a court appearance in a lawsuit in which his network was involved. It had taken up half the day, although his actual time in court was just a few minutes. The rest had been the anxious waiting through the procedures of the court. Afterward, he had called his wife, Lisa, to let her know that all had gone as well as expected. He had had to get back to the office and their conversation was brief and to the point. He came home that evening tired, direct from his studio without stopping for his usual quick drink. Lisa met him at the door and they kissed and exchanged a few pleasantries, but little more, as he prepared himself to relax for the evening. Just before sitting down to a customary Bloody Mary he remembered to call his lawyer.

It was his lawyer's wife who answered and told him

Charley had come home only moments before and was changing his clothes. She had heard a little about the case and asked Mike how it had gone. Mike then began an animated, joking conversation about it, elaborating on the fussiness of courtroom detail and reciting all sorts of amusing insights he held. Lisa watched silently from her kitchen stool but with mounting fury. Then after he hung up she began!

"Jesus, you barely mumble at me what happened, and I'm your wife, remember. I wait around here all day for you to come home. Then when you do get here, late as usual, you can't wait to get on the phone and tell someone else, someone you hardly know, like Myra, and fill her with jokes and charm. I can stand around here all night with a drink and a smile like a hostess at the bunny club until you deign to notice. If it was as funny as all that, why do I have to wait to overhear you while you tell it to someone else? Why is it you can be so entertaining to somebody else, anybody else, and just pass right by me? Have you just gotten tired of me? Is it that I'm not attractive to you any more? How can you be so thoughtless and inconsiderate?"

That started it. Mike knew Lisa had it in her to be bitchy, though in their seven years of marriage she was hardly as one-dimensional as that. Mostly she was a good deal sweeter and more understanding. And he wanted some of that part of her character after his long day. He countered with his explanation of "wanting to be civil with Charley's wife because I can never remember her first name" and progressed to accusing Lisa of not letting him relax when he came home in need of some escape from tension, not a heightening of it.

"Look, I'm tired after working all day trying to pull a few

ideas out of my brain and trying my best to satisfy impossible demands by useless people. I'm just not ready to come across with comedy. And suddenly, when I come home expecting quiet, and comfort, you turn around and demand to be entertained. You seem to want the TV and not me."

"That's right. You can just come home and take me for granted. I'll be here, waiting. You don't have to do anything. You can turn your charm on other people who really count. Now you don't even care what I think. You just want to make Myra laugh. You want her reaction. My response couldn't count for less!"

"You know damn well I'll get around to telling you what happened. Who else shares in my ideas and thoughts? Who do I test things out with? I never let anyone look at a half-baked, half-finished project. But if I'm stuck I let you in to my stuff even when it's pure chaos. But instead of what I have and want to give you—myself, whether strong or weak—you want someone else. Just now what I had was a tired self. But you won't have that. You want a stand-up comic!"

That was the way the fight started in one home. Where it went and how it ended, I'll leave to your imagination for the moment, because the possibilities are endless. For now, let's stay with the beginnings of it.

If you think you recognize something, a haunting ring of familiarity, a memory of your own experience, you're right. You should. Because the chances are you've been in countless scenes of fighting with your own lover that played like that one. Forget the words and listen to the music. Its theme is the one repeated and repeated through the fighting grown-up lovers normally do, repeated like an irritating musical line you can't forget. It remains in all the fighting lovers must endure. It occurs and recurs so consistently and often that finally the fighting itself, whatever the subject, whatever the content, whatever the style, serves only to assert this single unanswerable argument: "You don't love me as much (or as well) as I love you!"

Certainly it seems simplistic to reduce the myriad arguments of which we're capable as lovers to a single theme. But that, after all the hurly-burly is sifted down, after all the mess and complexity is carded over, is what it boils down to.

Yes, people fight over money. Over the in-laws, over the children, over anything and everything. But the issue is still the same. Endless variation in style, subject matter limited only by human imagination, intensity geared up or down according to our individual tastes. But our fights still say the same thing.

Stop the fight somehow, intervene between Mike and Lisa or their equivalents in your life, ask the lover-now-fighter from your position as fly-on-the-wall just how he feels, just what he is angry and fighting about. One lover claims his needs are neglected, another that his vulnerability is not respected, and another that the intimacies of the relationship are not protected. And yet another clamors it's his loving and himself that's been rejected.

And in spite of all complexity and the panoply of human form that give it variation, the message remains that one: "I love you, but you don't love me as well."

At closer range each lover feels the more alone. Isolated, misunderstood, betrayed, attacked—and separate. And justified in his anger. After all, at the core he feels his own availability and openness. Before him is his lover, closed in anger, leading an attack. And there must follow an immediate sense of the desertion, of being left alone in disappointment. It all began, as it usually does, with some little thing, some small expectation that the lover failed to meet. And now this, this hateful feeling, and a mounting of demands on both their parts, and a mounting heap of memories of the failing of them. The fight itself is making a demand. That all the implicit promises shall be fulfilled. The fight itself demands proof that it's not true, the very thing which each lover says by fighting—"I love you more than you are loving me."

It's an impossible, untenable situation. An impossible, unanswerable demand. Because it's true, for each of us, that in any given moment with our lover we love him more than he can love us back.

You've opened yourself up to loving closeness, invested in your lover all the dreams that childhood left unrealized, all the hopes that started off your loving, the wish for a world without a flaw, for a perfect answer to an imperfect question. How can he ever do all that? Make up for mother's failure and the rest, the failure of the lovers gone before, fulfill the dreams of innocence that you still dream. He fails—and you must know the world of all your loving has its limits. And you know your openness and your vulnerability. Suddenly there is a moment of self-shock. Like looking down, as in some nightmare of a full-dress party in your honor, to find yourself entirely unclothed. "Oh, my God!" And you run away to hide or turn and command that all remove their clothes. And *that* is the moment of risk.

Because it's not entirely possible to expect of your lover that he divest himself of defenses exactly at the same time and in the same manner as you do. You can coax. You can seduce. You can lead by example. But the demand you do make is for openness, for vulnerability that's as great as yours. So that your lover may join you in your sense of desolation, to make up somehow for the loss you feel in knowing that the loving's been imperfect—to keep you from waking from your dream.

But the demand for openness in the name of love is no more possible to fulfill than the demand for love itself. And yet, that's just what lovers do demand of each other. "You don't love me as much as I love you—because if you did, you would . . . you wouldn't . . ." And the disappointment. The anger mounting.

As the recipient of such demands, you feel their violation, the sense of their intrusion into your boundaries, the expectation that you'll comply with giving or, in your openness, forgo your demands. And you feel his wishes as assault. You see it all as an attempt to gain dominion, to compromise your willing weakness by taking power and control. You see yourself commanded to surrender, give up the choice of what you'll be and do, give up the sweetest virtues of adulthood, to one whose claim on you is love. And you'll be damned! And you attack. And you retreat a little in your loving, to take care of the wound you feel in the demands your lover makes and in your own sweet reasonable requests frustrated. And you fight like hell to save yourself from this.

Small wonder it needs only some little thing, an almost insignificant stimulus, a letter that wasn't mailed on time, an oversight in simple conversation, some overlooking of each other's feelings, a casual comment meant to tease that really hurts. And the fight begins. This one fact is puzzling to the lovers and even more to those professionals they ask to help them in their plight. The serious battles of loving begin over the most trifling of matters, incidents, and comments that later all agree should have had no weight. But the intensity that builds from them is hardly insignificant. It can lead to the wish to murder and occasionally to the reality of it.

What does it mean that the fight begins over some little nothing? It should tell us that the *actual* reason for the battle is not the *true* cause. That unmailed letter can't, alone, explain the mayhem that was brought about in its name. Perhaps, then, this bit of trivia is just a straw breaking the camel's back. Well, then, we ought to know what the camel's burden was to begin with.

The fact that it takes very little to start the fighting between lovers highlights the vulnerability that must remain with loving in the first place, part of the consequence of openness and expectation, trust given and wishes generated. The small precipitant is just a signal that the balance of the loving is unstable for that moment, that there is shift between the love of self felt as autonomy and the loving of another. And each movement back and forth threatens one boundary or another, the boundary of the self-space or the boundary of the relationship toward which so much of one's self-love has been extended.

The shift may have begun through some change in either of the lovers, or in the relationship itself, through some event outside it. Perhaps, even before the fight began, even before that small precipitating incident, one lover began to feel a bit more vulnerable, began to sense some threat to his autonomy, began to feel a little anxious over the maintaining of his boundaries. It may have started elsewhere, through some experience in the world at large, the world of friends and strangers, or in his inner world, his private universe of thought and feeling, fantasy and mood, dream and impulse. Or some event within his own body. A change in any of these worlds that impinge on and make up, in their effect, the boundaries of the union of the lovers, a change pure and simple, acting, by the mere fact of its occurrence, to alter that boundary, to alter the distance one way or another between the lovers.

Whatever gave rise to it, as a result he began to feel more open, vulnerable, and anxious. Had he been aware of his internal rumblings, able to communicate the state of his experience, in a listenable fashion, had his partner been available and able to listen and provide the right support, and in a manner and degree that both could find acceptable, the whole thing might have been averted. Unpleasantness might not have come between them. But all those "if's" make a very fragile barrier. And since it's likely that at some point one of the contingencies would go unfulfilled, the final matter, a casual comment, an unintended look, needs only to be a reminder of the separation he begins to feel already. Like that first atom's split in a chain reaction.

Let's look at a typical fight as it begins:

HARRY: Have you seen that little notebook around here someplace?

SHIRLEY: No, I haven't. Why? (*Looks up from her magazine.*)

HARRY: Because I need it and badly. It's got an important phone number I have to call before tomorrow.

SHIRLEY: Well, it will turn up. (*She returns to her magazine and continues reading.*)

HARRY: Not around here it won't. Goddamn it. (*Shirley continues to read in silence. Harry stomps around with increasing loudness.*) Goddamn it! Shit! Why can't I ever find anything in this goddamn place?

SHIRLEY: (*Looking up.*) Because you never put anything away is why.

HARRY: Well, aren't you smug? Why don't you do something? Why don't you get off your butt and help me instead of jabbering? That phone number is for arranging a guy to estimate putting in your new kitchen. Get it? *Your* new kitchen.

SHIRLEY: (*Not moving.*) Well, if you'd pick up after yourself you'd find things, not lose them.

HARRY: Goddamn it, this house is such a sloppy mess all the time it's a wonder I can find you. Come to think of it, I never can.

SHIRLEY: That's because every spare minute I have after teaching school all day is spent doing errands and stuff for you.

HARRY: If you put in a little more time cleaning, this place would be in better shape and I wouldn't be chasing my tail off finding numbers for your kitchen.

SHIRLEY: Look! You're such a messy creep, you wouldn't notice if I cleaned every day, or if I never cleaned. As it happens, I clean every day and quite a bit of it is your junk. And I deserve some consideration.

HARRY: Oh, Christ! I try to be thoughtful—I get hung. If I try to ask you what's bothering you, I get it in the head. What does a guy have to do to satisfy you?

SHIRLEY: Just try a little thoughtfulness, Harry, just try a little. Stop thinking only of number one.

Once Harry and Shirley have gotten to this point, they usually have forgotten whatever it was that provoked things.

They are beginning to feel some sense of injury and a feeling of righteousness that combine to stoke the fire of their anger. What may continue to fuel that fire are any old smolders of resentment hanging around from their past living together. And if their fighting style includes throwing in those old embers, they can generate enough heat to burn up everything they've built together.

If somehow we could have an instant replay of a quarrel, if, even more, we could run the lives of the lovers back in time through the hours before the fight began, we would have the missing pieces to the puzzle. We would be able to see the moment when each person began to feel some threat to his integrity, some tension in his boundaries. Then if we played the argument over, speeded up so that those feelings that preceded it could be included, we might get something like this.

SHIRLEY: (*To herself.*) I'm just feeling lousy. Must be my period coming, that full, bloated feeling. Uugh! And still so many things to do before Harry gets here. When he does he probably won't notice whether the house is clean or not.

HARRY: Hi, honey. I'm home. Boy did I have a rough day!

SHIRLEY: I'm sorry to hear that. Look, Harry, I'm really feeling cruddy today. I'd like to just sit instead of rushing dinner.

HARRY: Oh? What's the matter? The kids in your class give you a rough time?

SHIRLEY: It's nothing.

HARRY: It's never nothing. C'mon, what's on your mind?

SHIRLEY: Nothing! I just feel ugly is all. Can't a person feel bad by themselves?

HARRY: O.K. Pardon me for asking. I won't bother you, then. Why don't you just stay there with your magazine. I'll go make a phone call.

(*Five minutes later.*)

HARRY: (*Coming in to the living room, visibly annoyed.*)
Have you seen that little notebook around here someplace?

SHIRLEY: No, I haven't. Why?

And the fight's on. And where and how it goes depends upon the style these lovers set, their rules for fighting, spoken and implicit.

My colleagues and I, in Boston, have been successfully using the idea of replaying fights and what precedes them in videotapes of couples and families. Some of the people who have agreed to be the subject of our studies, and to share with us and with the camera the privacy of their coping, have come for help because their own felt pain was too great to carry alone. Others presented themselves to us because of their wish to learn more about themselves. In either case, the experience has proved not only useful from a therapeutic standpoint but invaluable as a rich source of the materials that stimulated this book.

We are, of course, hardly alone in our interest in families. But a systematic attention has not been extensively paid to conflict and fighting in the family, even by the professional family therapists. An important exception is the work of Dr. George Bach and his co-workers in California, as elaborated in the book *The Intimate Enemy*. They have devised some useful techniques for helping people to use their fights constructively.

When we first began our work with families, we assumed, as apparently did Dr. Bach and most professionals, that fighting was some kind of symptom of trouble, a measure of "ill health" in a relationship, a sign that something was "wrong," and we also assumed, implicitly, that if that something could be righted, the result would be the abatement of the fighting. While much that is essentially useful could be and was learned from this approach, I find now that it was largely wrong, that far from being symptomatic of an illness in a marriage, fighting tells us that the love's alive and well.

Fighting is, of course, unpleasant for most of us, and it and its residues create much pain. The wish to cure or to relieve by making pain go away is one result of medical training. It is also easier to look for what is wrong in a complex living thing than to look for what is right about it. Especially when what is right *appears* by all its qualities of disruption to be the very paradigm of what we expect to be wrong.

And so we designed techniques for teaching people *how* to fight. We tried to help them to make structure out of chaos. One way is to give the fight a focus, a central issue that both people try to keep in mind throughout the fight, and to try thereby to keep the substance of the fighting clearly limited. That method sets a limit on those complex hassles people create that go everywhere and do nothing, that create pain and are so diffuse that everything gets dragged in, including the kitchen sink, but nothing much is accomplished and, what is worse, in the confusion nothing much is understandable or understood.

Another guide is to set limits on the time allowed for fighting. The purpose here is to create closure, a pressure to be over and be done. And to curtail those battles without limit that often seem to result in exhaustion and nothing more.

Another is the setting of a goal, an idea of a positive outcome, a change, however small, that each hopes to achieve in the relationship.

And yet another is explicit ground rules, behavior that

is tolerable, behavior that is not. This, in an effort to control the style of fighting and keep the partners safe from each other.

All these guidelines and the others we devised, or that were designed by other well-intentioned, experienced therapists, do have a usefulness. Especially when people lose so much control that there is danger of great harm, or simply when they do not know how to carry on an argument.

But the problem is that all the rules in the world, however well-intentioned, will not cover the contingencies that happen normally, somewhere between these extremes. In other words, most of us already have our rules, or we can learn a few new ones, but it still won't alter our situation. That we experience only the pain of all our quarrels and mostly we would like to find another way.

Because in spite of ourselves we share with the rule-makers the conviction that fighting is somehow a bad thing. The rules work to convert a fight to an argument. To make an essentially emotional, potentially explosive process into a cooler, limited, partially intellectual one.

Although it may be necessary to do this for some people, or necessary to make rules to help us, as therapists, in our struggle with the chaos before us, in the end the rules must be discarded, serving as they do to constrict us and keep us a prisoner of our biases, unable to explore the benefit the fight may bring. Rules, for most of us, take the *goodness* out of the fight.

Fighting is an *inevitable* and *healthy* and *sexually stimulating* punctuation of a *good* marriage, of any good and happy loving. And yes, carried far enough, it can be dangerous to your health. Well, we are getting inured to lives of danger. The necessary life-giving functions are becoming risky daily and that doesn't stop us. Even breathing has an element of danger—that doesn't stop our breathing.

I've already said so much about the necessity for anger in a loving relationship and for its expression, *directly* within the relationship, that it seems unnecessary to add anything about the inevitability of fighting. Yet, even now, I can't overstress the view that fighting is a sign of life, not death, in a relationship.

In the midst of life, to make loving possible, it may be necessary to accept the painful reality of fighting. Some realities must simply be borne, however painful, because they cannot be eluded. The knowledge of inevitability invites a "soft" surrender, one without the additionally crippling burden of anxiety. Like falling down gracefully when you're skiing, for example.

For many of us, it may be necessary that we assume just that fatalistic tolerance toward fighting and anger in order to bear it. Because nobody looks forward to their next battle with a lover. But learning the usefulness of fighting may go far toward making it acceptable. Or any other separation or threat of separation in loving.

When you love someone, you want them with you always, you want to be with them always. You seek to establish that dream of loving that the first love with mother promised but did not fulfill in actuality. This time you will make it happen. You want it so much that separation is unthinkable. And any threat of separation brings anxiety. And yet, for adults, that is just what's necessary, if you're to have a growing and a sexual love. You must let go in order to keep your lover.

Letting go is the key to keeping the relationship alive. You give up your lover in order to keep his love and your loving alive. You give him up to his work, to your children, to interests outside the bounds of what you share. To friends and family, other people that he loves. And finally, you must give him up to himself.

But letting go is not easy. It goes against the instincts. It is an attitude that may develop over time, not of resignation or surrender, but of acceptance of the stranger and his real needs apart from you.

Fighting helps to bring that acceptance about. And that's what I mean by its contribution to the health of the relationship. People like to talk about their relationship. But ask them to define it, to tell you just what it is—and they are at a loss. They can't tell you because they are too close to it for that kind of perspective. But they can and do define their relationship, *in action*, when they fight and thereby re-create the space that is potentially between them. That gives them the perspective to look at each other and what they share in their union.

The good fight in loving re-establishes each lover as an independent person with his own integrity. It re-creates a capsule of living through a total loss of loving, as in a death. And the lovers, each, endure those feelings of a loss, the mixture of longing and hatred. But in this case its not the finality of death; it's possible to bring the lover back through loving and through letting him go at the same time.

Sexual longing and sexual activity arise and once again reduce the space between the lovers to almost nothingness.

Fighting happens to make the loving and the lovers new again.

And this alternation of feeling and action, of loving and hating, of fighting and fucking, works to keep things straight with the marriage, to keep the lovers real to each other and whole to themselves. It happens through the stress that operates at the boundaries, and through the building of those defensive barriers which each fight makes happen. At the same time the loving which is there, as well, makes it possible for those boundaries to be more inclusive, more expanded with each episode of unwanted, painful experience of anger. That's the growth in it for lovers. They're more real to each other afterward. They're a little more capable of loving each other as separate beings, people with a right to their own feelings and needs, their own life, and their own death.

Sex can then recur out of the space that fighting has made possible.

And start the whole thing on to the next cycle of its growth.

Or sex can occur out of the fighting itself. More than one couple has learned that lovemaking that follows a fight is "somehow" better. And quite often they'll admit, shamefacedly, that the truth of the "somehow" is that it was the fight itself that "turned them on," especially if the fight included some physical violence—a strong gesture of touching, of slapping, of biting at the lover's body—that began in hatred and the wish to tear everything apart and ended in a new loving and a coming together.

Sex can arise from fighting partly because the body is a conservative system and it uses the same basic mechanisms to carry the messages that spell love and hate. The bodily changes in sexual arousal are strikingly similar to those in preparation for combat. What I hope is clear is that the combination of our "unimaginative" bodily coping and our very active imaginings of threat to our integrity make necessary the stances that we assume at first encounter and that we resume at any separation or the threat of it. And that, together, the sense of distance and separation created by the anger and the physical excitement generated in it, make it comparatively easy to convert a battle royal to a royal bedroom scene.

I said that it is usually with some embarrassment that lovers will admit their sex was good after a fight. That's because they are, like all of us, victims of our insight. We've all become the victims of our psychological moralizing; we've been taught to think that anyone who gets a sex kick out of beating somebody is weird. That sort of thing is supposedly perverse, according to our diagnosis awarders. It's associated with special leather clothes, whips, torture chambers, and the wonderful historic names Marquis de Sade and Sacher-Masoch. De Sade, through his writings and supposed activities, gave his name to a so-called perversion in which the *main sexual pleasure* is derived from beating, torturing, dominating someone—hence, "sadism." The companion pleasure, in being beaten, tortured, or dominated, took its name from the second gentleman and his practices—thus, "masochism."

I don't want to hang us up here on any extensive consideration of perversions, except to set the record straight for those who are nervous about that good loving they had this weekend just after slamming each other around a little. If there is something which we could all agree to label as perversion in sexual behavior, its primary quality would reside in its absence of choice. The perverse which we can or *insist* we can recognize has elements of fixity, of rigidity, without variation. It partakes of that inflexibility that makes us see the action as "driven." Now that kind of definition of perversion includes under its umbrella a great many people who would never permit themselves to deviate, in matters sexual, from heterosexual intercourse in the face-to-face, man-above, woman-below "missionary position."

No, I'm not talking about extremists of any type here. Just the plain folks we all know who, occasionally, in their own privacy begin a fight with angry words that give way to angry hands. When the bodies' sting begun by those slaps reverberates and the heat and the sensation of suddenness, of brilliant sharp aliveness, arouse other feelings of sexual aliveness. And before they know they don't care about the *winning* of that argument.

Even at the final moments of sexual joining, the hating feelings don't just vanish. They wanted to tear something apart. And "somehow" it is each other's clothes.

Somehow that one violation, the physical one, of slapping at each other's flesh, generates the excitement that ends in penetrating each other's bodies. And somehow too, the physical intrusion makes real and limits the threat of forced entry to the lovers' emotional space. Loving is threatening to those boundaries. And the fight's been about the inner sensing of the threat, the feeling of vulnerability, of being open and without control—all stated so succinctly in the words "You don't love me as much as I love you." And then the first hand crosses, the first slap lands, then another returns, and back, and maybe a kick, a scratch or two. And each discovers there are limits to their vulnerability. Here it is, the worst of it. The beating. But there is also the beating back. The sure knowledge that there are some things that won't be tolerated. That neither one is simply lying on his back as if to say, "Go ahead, do anything you want." (Unless, of course, this does happen to be that singular match of the true sadist and the true masochist.)

Sexuality bridges gaps. And loving closeness, much as we

yearn for it, threatens boundaries, stresses our autonomy. But violence beforehand is like an insurance. It is a telling of the other that you're really separate, in the very feeling of your smarting skin. The loving closeness has become a threat, a fear that you will overwhelm each other, penetrate, engulf each other's innards. Now it's clear, when those hands slap out, that it's *only* a *threat*. That in the violence dealt out, met and responded to, you and your lover reassure yourselves of your abilities to ward each other off. And having each survived intact, through the fighting and the violence, you can permit again the closeness of the sex and the loving.

The love and hate of lovers and of loving can run together even less dramatically. In play the lovers bite each other, tease each other, pinch or punch each other. All in fun. With no thought that play is just another word for bringing life creatively out of the dead earnest. This play is a way of bringing into manageable form the difficult tensions and overboiling feelings that the conflict of distance and closeness generates. You want to be tender and hurting at the same time.

The fact that sex and violence are so intimately related in our bodies has its practical side for helping those who do get caught on one side of their ambivalence.

Here's what I mean:

Bob is just 30. Hardly an age when a man expects to have a waning in his sexual interest. But that's just what was bringing him to see me. He had been divorced for four years now, and had had several unsuccessful sexual relationships since the end of his marriage. In all of them and in his marriage itself, he had trouble maintaining an erection long enough to have intercourse. Now he was seeing a girl he really liked. They were openly discussing the possibility of future sex between them and Bob was worried.

In his case, as in so many others, the original trouble with erection seemed to have been a minor difficulty which grew in scope as he worried about it. And gradually as he did worry and his wife became less and less sympathetic, he became more and more impotent. Finally they both decided to give up. And parted.

In trying to help him with his current situation I needed to know lots about his past, and he gave a long and complex history of family trouble centering on his father's alcoholism and his mother's controlling nature. But the most enlightening bit of data was the description of one of the few times he and his wife, Cynthia, managed to have satisfactory sex.

"I was out shoveling snow. It was a hell of a snowfall and I must have been out there for pretty near two hours. I was tired. My muscles were aching from lifting that wet snow. And I was sweating and getting cold at the same time, so finally I went in. Cindy was there, waiting for me, with a drink. She had changed her clothes and taken a bath. She was dressed in a nightgown thing. I almost didn't bother to notice her except that when I took my clothes off I suddenly had an erection. I was kind of surprised myself. And then at how easy it all was. We just made love there and then right next to my clothes on the bedroom rug and it was terrific. It all just happened so naturally that time. I still don't understand it. And I never did repeat it with her just like that."

Or there are Carl and Betty. Remember them? The desperate, hand-holding Beautiful Couple who wondered after ten years of marriage if that was all there was to life.

They claimed that neither could be "turned on" by the other and they chose not to look outside their marriage. What they saw by looking carefully *at* their marriage was a steady pattern of conflicts avoided for the sake of sweet reason, a complicity to maintain peace at any price.

But sometimes even the best of conspiracies must fail. And when theirs did give way, even momentarily to some out-and-out quarrel over trifles, they would find themselves suddenly attracted and, as quickly, in bed together.

Bob as well as Carl and Betty had accidently tapped on the key to help with their problems. Their easy conversion of aggression and sexuality tells us that what was missing from their sex lives before was some way to allow them to experience and express that uncomfortable anger.

That sounds a great deal simpler than it is in practice, since, if it were so easy, they wouldn't have needed my help in the first place. The permission to be oneself, comfortable with one's aggression, covers a lot of territory. For Bob it was important to look at his fears of being dominated, swallowed up by a woman, and to help him cope with those fears and their origin in his upbringing, watching a father invalid himself with his wife's tender help. It was more than simply telling him to do exercise prior to sexual relations, some spectacle of a man rushing off to do calisthenics in a madcap speeded-up Keystone Kop frenzy—and then leaping into bed. But even that would be a start. Some means, even the artificial one of deliberate exercise, to start the juices of sex and aggression flowing.

For Carl and Betty their very definite issues of establishing a distance in their relationship compatible with closeness, yet not yielding in their individual autonomy, could be resolved for the moment through a good fight. Like a great many people oversold on "togetherness," frightened of their own anger and afraid of what they have been taught is "sickness" in their fighting, this couple's "peace at any price" needed undermining if they were to find ways to create and tolerate separation within their loving and directly to be comfortably angry. They needed permission to express that anger, even physically, violently, as a release from their tensions and as a striking point for sex. The simple accessibility of sex after fighting makes it possible for them to renew their involvement while the work of firming up the rest of the marriage's foundation goes on. Serious questions of trust must be dealt with. After all, where anger has been so mutually avoided, where is the trust these two need to feel? Can you trust someone with whom you cannot be yourself? Can you really trust someone with whom you can't expose your anger? And the difficult process of repair is helped by the realization they have come to, themselves, that there *is* a benefit to their fighting. And the obvious proof is in their memory of sex together afterward.

And it's equally obvious to those who have suffered the experience that even the benefit of anger in sexual excitement can sometimes fail to match its destructiveness. Fighting certainly can be a risky business.

More than bruised egos, hurt feelings, there is the risk to limb and life. The national crime statistics identify murders and serious violence that just falls short of murder as mostly crimes of kinship. Most of the time the violent scene involves people who have some sort of long-standing involvement. Often violence is a family affair.

You've heard it said that most accidents happen in the

home. That's probably true largely because home is where people spend a great deal of their time, and usually people drop whatever caution they habitually exercise outside and so are least prepared to think of danger when they're home. The same can be said for murders and near murders. Most of them happen in the context of closeness, between people with some pre-established tie.

You may have had fantasies sometime, reading of this sensational murder, that report of a riot, or of the general upsurge of violence in the country, that some unknown person, a stranger, could well accost or threaten you or even put your life in danger. You may even have a mental image of this would-be assailant. If you've gone even further, perhaps you've indentified your would-be attacker as poor or crazed, but a stranger. At the most exotic he looks like a horror out of a Frankenstein movie.

Put it away. If anyone ever does put your life in jeopardy, it probably won't be a stranger. It is much more likely to be someone with whom you have smiled, broken bread, or shared the intimacies of bed.

Take Frank and Sally. Both respectable people in their fifties, both with responsible positions in the community. Who would know from looking at their smooth and charming exterior that here was a couple on the point of divorce because the mayhem they created in their fighting seemed to have no limit—not even murder?

According to Frank, Sally was smothering him and trying to choke him, literally and figuratively. Sally complained that now, after marrying her lover, he would strike her hand away when she just reached out to touch him. And her persistence in reaching out to Frank netted only the reward of a kick in the rump.

Their problems in establishing some kind of tolerable space between them were so great that they often used violence as a means to resolve them. Each had been married before and had had children, now grown up. Before they were married and actually living together, things had seemed to be working out fine. Now, two years after the wedding, and countless battles later, the marriage was at the point of ending. Frank liked to get off by himself and had arranged his life and his work to give him plenty of time for it. Sally felt panicky when he left her alone and made increasing demands on him for support, especially for physical contact. Frank felt that she was trapping him, confining him. He felt that he now had to account to Sally for each minute that had been his alone. Their actual fights would begin with some trivial event or an accusing angry comment about a previous battle. Frank would usually stew, gradually building up a head of steam and growing furious. This apparent detachment increased Sally's anxious need for a kind or forgiving word and she would only increase the intensity of her carping.

Finally he would leave the room, storming out to cool his temper, afraid of what he might do to her if he stayed. She would follow him from room to room. He would try to leave the house. She would take his things in ransom, his glasses, his car keys, even his clothes. Finally the escalator would stop and Frank would "blow," slapping her, and when she kicked at him, he would respond by punching her. If the fight didn't lead to a rushed visit to the hospital, it might end by their going silently to bed, where Sally would move toward Frank for some consolation and forgiveness in his touch. Frank, in turn, would find himself "turned off" at this point. From his standpoint, anger beyond a certain point extinguished his sexual feelings. Sally, too, admitted that it was not sex but comfort she was after, in the aftermath of the battle. For this couple, the troubles they had establishing a working distance in all areas of their marriage, without resorting to uncontrolled rage, could not be resolved in the bedroom. It could only be aggravated there because the mutual sense of threat was so extreme.

The insult and the injury of violence is not always and only dealt out through the body's pain. Not only through the tearing of the flesh. There is the injury of the spirit, sometimes as great or greater, when the cruel words tear through another's barriers, tear apart his sense of self, tread viciously on just those points of weakness that were willingly exposed before, in the name of love, in living and loving together. That tearing of each other's standards, the breaking of each other's self-respect, that violence may be the greater injury. Leaving behind a wound that in the end is fatal to the relationship. Because each one feels somehow lessened in it. Reduced in value. Diminished in his sense of self.

The anger that can do such violence to tissue and to inner feeling must reflect so great a threat in closeness and a corresponding need so great that people like this do their best loving at a distance. Removed where there can be no touching and no fear of being overwhelmed. They may have wonderful affairs but be unable to sustain the everyday breakdowns of boundaries that are a part, and a necessary part, of marriage.

We've come full circle, then, from Lucille and her terrifying fear of men, her overwhelming need of them, and how it kept her distant from the outset, to Frank and Sally, whose threatened selfhood in their loving and living makes the violence in behavior finally real. The threat of love, of closeness, the need for it, become so great that Lucille violently resists the *coming together* and Frank and Sally can't go through with *making it*. For these people, too, the rules may not work. Clearly they need help to deal with anger, but in the process life goes on, and a marriage founders or relationships never even start. It's here I'd say some people ought better avoid marriage entirely, or, while they struggle to find themselves in hope of sometime later being whole and ready, they might seek mates who can live and love at great distance.

What about the rest of us, the non-violent ones? Well, we can learn some too. That there are limits. Limits to what marriage will be able to accept and give, limits on our tolerance, limits, certainly, to what therapy can do.

And how do you know when you've passed beyond the limits?

How do you know when your anger is *only* destructive? Or your violence in action and in attitude, body and spirit, deed and word, is too much? It is when you exceed the limits that exist between you in your loving. And in truth, how you know is impossible to answer in more than generalities because, obviously, the limits vary for the people involved. But if you've been following this whole argument, one thing should have emerged: the purpose of anger (or, better, its usefulness), whatever its form of expression (the accent is on *ex*-pression—insidious and stifled anger gone underground to emerge in another shape will do little that is good), is to provide *safe* distance, re-establish boundaries, reaffirm individual lovers' autonomous being. This can't be at the cost of life, or limb, or self-respect, or sanity, or even, really, of love. When the hating is on you, and you are blinded bullshit with its furies, tenderness may seem far from your mind. But it must come back, sometime. It's lingering hatreds that are the most destructive. The hero in the movie *Morgan* said it: "Violence lends dignity to a loving man!" Dignity. But to a *loving* man. Or woman.

Dignity in loving. That is the feeling that enables you to *let go*, to let go of your lover in the many ways you know he needs to be himself. It allows you the generosity to give him back to himself. To create in the many small moments of living the separations sexual loving needs—by letting him go. Hoping and knowing he'll come back to you in free will. And it permits you to let go of yourself, your passions openly explosive in a friendly rage, to dump, when the moment's ripe for it, a full bowl of salad in his lap. And really start the good fight going.

6

Where Did the Prince Go? What the Hell Is This Frog Doing Here?

WE ARE THE VICTIMS of our *expectations*. And the hapless prey of the culture's myths. And in the case of our own modern culture, the mythmaking on a vast scale by media experts ties us by unhappy accident to the wheel of our society's consumer-production-exploitation machinery. The Great American Dream Machine. A vast creative network busily pouring out films and songs and plays which function to keep us busily turning the wheel, keeping the society and the culture spinning. Nowhere is the discrepancy between actual living experience and the dream of it which we have been taught to accept as real more painfully and acutely felt than in the everyday experience of involvement with another, the long-term "committed" relationship. Our Dream Machine has churned out fantasy after fantasy which prepares us for the ecstatic, the acme experience. We await with longing the falling in love, the being in love. We've been taught to believe in rapture, in joy, in delirium. What a comedown it is from being in love to being in life.

Because, of course, living is not a continuous ecstasy. No

nervous system could stand the wear and tear of constant orgasm. Living together is not even loving all the time. Instead it is complex, an ebbing and flowing, even of loving feelings. It is an admixture of loving and hating feelings. It is even an unawareness of feelings, a withdrawal of feelings. It is all these and more at one time and another. It is in large measure mundane. It is everyday.

This is not to put down love. It is not to coat life with cynicism. It is to set things right. Most of us are so used to taking our cues for reality from the edited images of a movie that we are more than a little disappointed by the rough, unretouched version that our living must be. We see the great love of two superstar idols before us on the screen and hope and dream that we can have the same, be the same as they. And when we don't get our dreams fulfilled, we feel cheated.

The artifice behind the art has played us merry. How often are we shown the small irritations of the lives we watch and learn from? When does a great screen lover wait for a bus? Suffer menstrual cramps? Endure broken telephone connections? Wait for a restaurant table?

They don't have limitations. Or when they do it is part of the script, written grandly with suffering as beautiful as the rest of the carefully contrived plot. When is a beautiful film goddess shown waiting regularly and alone for someone to call for a date? And without a background of a thousand crying violins?

Believing, we are unprepared for a life without soundtracks. We are unprepared to recognize the goodness of what we have because, in comparison to what we know in the darkness of our theater seats, it is nothing. Not good enough. We are prepared to accept constant and ecstatic loving and nothing else!

Compared to the images on our own inner dream screens, ghost-scripted by the impressions we have learned from Hollywood's labor, real life seems worse than paltry. And the true struggle of any loving commitment feels like a confidence game.

Any myth worthy of the name fulfills its function only when it helps to support the deepest wishes of our dreams or when it helps to deny that which we most fear. We certainly do not want to face the fact that love is finite, mutable, and not everlasting. We want to believe just the opposite. Erich Segal wrote the classic cliché line for the movie/book *Love Story*, saying, "Love means not ever having to say you're sorry." And as one patient put it, "Real love is when love is there all the time."

Only "incredible" can describe the fantasies that underlie these vain hopes. What makes them truly sad is that somewhere, in our fashion, each of us has a secret nurtured cliché of his own that probably does these one better. How can we believe that love is when you never have to say "I'm sorry"? Or that love can "be there all the time"? Only when we denigrate ourselves and our full humanity. For only in the absence of human conflict, human anger, human injustice, and human regret is there no need for human forgiveness. And instead of loving constantly and continually, the best our human selves can do is to experience the other intermittently, to cherish and to love, over and above simply acknowledging his or her existence, with intensity varying from time to time and with an admixture of the opposite feelings of anger and contempt.

The fact is that were it not for this pattern, one of undulation, of change, of backing and filling, in our loving, no relationship, however apparently loving, would go anywhere. No growth would be possible in the two people or in the relationship that represents what is between them. Just as with individual development, where conflict and its resolution are a necessary catalyst for learning, so in couples and more extended involvements, the failures in loving, its lapses, its opposite, hating, are part of the yeast of growth. That is what is meant by learning through trial and error. Without error, there is no learning. And how we all resist learning!

That's what our myth tells us about ourselves. We would like to stop, to rest, maybe to be still. If we cannot do this in our own selves, in our singleness, in our individual lonely lives, perhaps we can find some other, whose constant loving will liberate us from the ever-increasing pace of change and growth. Take us out of time. And the threat of death at its end.

Accepting our mortality allows us to learn to value what we have now, in the present, the only life we can ever fully know. And to value that loving we experience, however imperfect and mercurial, as the only reasonable palliative force, the one experience that lifts us momentarily from our aloneness. How sweet does this life and this love become when we accept the knowledge that it will end someday.

And that is the basis of our commitment to it. That we care in spite of everything, in spite of its failure to fulfill our myths and dreams. Because it is real and worthy of investment, and in spite of all our hopes and myths and dreams, it can only last for so short a time.